MW00379886

Professional
Coach
Training

Professional Coach Training

Developing Ministry Excellence and Effectiveness

A COACHING4CLERGY TEXTBOOK

By J. Val Hastings, MCC

Phone: 610-385-8034

Email: val@coaching4clergy.com

Web Site: www.coaching4clergy.com

Copyright © 2011 Coaching4Clergy and J. Val Hastings. All rights reserved. No part of this publication shall be reproduced or transmitted in any form or by any electronic, mechanical, photocopying or recording means, or otherwise, including information storage and retrieval systems, without permission in writing from the copyright holder.

ISBN 978-0-9886128-0-8

Published in the USA

Table of Contents

Acknowledgements

I am one of the lucky ones!

I am one of those individuals who has been surrounded by people that bring out the best in me. This book is dedicated to those who have empowered me as a person, a pastor and a professional coach.

I grew up with parents that encouraged me to pursue my dreams – and to dream big. I remember, as a child, telling them that I wanted to be a farmer, fireman, professional athlete, astronaut and pastor. And they told me to go for it. Thank you, Mom and Dad, for the years of encouragement that you have offered me.

My wife, Wendy, continually encourages me to pursue my dreams! How great to have a partner who wants the best for me. Thank you for your support and encouragement. What a gift you have given me.

To my two daughters, Bryanna and Shelby, you are my source of pride and joy. It's great being your Dad and helping you dream big and live out your dreams.

We've got a great team and faculty at Coaching4Clergy. I appreciate your commitment to our global vision and your contributions to this book.

To my Online Business Manager and Virtual Assistant, Laura Pumo, and her team at Office DEVA, thank you for pulling this all together for me. Your assistance was invaluable.

To all of the pastors, ministry staff and church leaders that I have coached and trained, this book is filled with what you have taught me. Others will benefit from you.

Val

Introduction

In 1999 I met my first coach. I'm embarrassed to say this, but my initial response to her was, "What sport do you coach?" After her light laughter, she explained to me that she coached individuals and organizations. I was intrigued. That intrigue has grown over the years into a global vision. The vision is that every spiritual leader has coach training in their professional toolkit. Your participation in this coach training event is helping this vision become a reality.

You may be wondering the motivation behind my vision. Like many of you, I am aware of the growing number of spiritual leaders who are ready to give up or feel ineffective and overwhelmed. Add to this the alarming number of today's churches that are closing, or near closing.

Actually, there's a reason behind all of this. We are in the midst of a paradigm shift involving a shift away from of the pastor-led (denominational-centered) approach to ministry and a shift toward the next great awakening in Christianity—the empowerment of all of God's people.

A coaching approach to ministry is one way to embrace this paradigm shift. It can have a tremendous impact, not only on the leaders of our faith communities, but also on the larger communities that we serve. The coaching skills contained in this textbook will help you gain greater clarity about who God is inviting you to become as an individual and as a faith community, as this paradigm shift unfolds.

Whether you are an ordained or non-ordained, paid or unpaid leader in your faith community, coaching is an extremely valuable and useful tool. At its core, coaching is about empowering others. What if empowering and equipping people became the norm in your faith community? Consider the impact that your faith community could have locally and globally.

Whatever (or whoever) motivated you to learn more about coaching, I want to thank you for taking this step. You are beginning a journey that will add tremendously to your life and the lives of others.

Congratulations! Let's begin.

Chapter One

Getting Started as a Coach

WHAT IS COACHING?

When people discover that I am a coach, they usually ask me what coaching is. As I start to explain, I usually observe a combination of confusion and intrigue in my listener's expression. Coaching, while powerful and transformational, is hard for many to understand. One person has told me on several occasions that she believes that the real reason people hire me as their coach is because they like the way my voice sounds on the phone. Others have hired me as their coach saying, "I don't know what coaching is, but whatever you did for _____ (another pastor), I want you to do for me."

I still chuckle at one pastor's response to my explanation of coaching: "So let me get this straight. You're going to do lots of listening, you're not going to tell me what to do nor are you going to try to fix me. I'm going to do all the work AND I'm going to pay you. I don't think so!"

Over the years I've discovered that the best way to help someone understand coaching is to give them a firsthand experience. That's why I give a LIVE demonstration at the beginning of every coach training event that I facilitate. Then I invite the participants to define what coaching is, based on what they have just witnessed.

And so, in addition to reading this manual, I invite you to experience your own demonstration of coaching by scheduling a complimentary coaching session. Not only is that the best way to understand coaching, you will also benefit from being coached. All of our Coaching4Clergy coaches offer these complimentary sessions with no strings attached; you'll find them listed on the Find-A-Coach Service on our website: www.Coaching4Clergy.com.

Let's define what coaching is and what it is not. The International Coach Federation (www.coachfederation.org) defines coaching as "partnering with clients in a thought-provoking and creative process that inspires them to maximize their personal and professional potential."

Here is how I define coaching: As a coach, I help people get the results they want by bringing out the best in them. Coaching isn't about fixing people or solving problems; coaching is a developmental or discovery-based process. Similar to athletic coaches, we further develop the skill and talent already inherent in the people we coach.

Whether you use the International Coach Federation definition of coaching, my definition or develop your own, there are several key components that I want to highlight:

1. **Coaching is a partnership.**
    The coach and the coachee are involved in a collaborative process that is 100% about the person being coached. The relationship between the coach and coachee is of utmost importance. Safety and trust in this relationship create an environment in which fresh perspectives and new ways of being can be explored. Coachees are more likely to let you see who they really are if they believe that they can trust you.

    This is so important for today's spiritual leaders, many of whom report that they are extremely lonely and feel isolated. In fact, on more than one occasion, I've had pastors report that there is no one they trust, nor anyone they feel close to. If nothing else, the rise of coaching in faith communities will provide today's spiritual leaders with a safe person to talk with. And that's a big win!

2. **Coaching accelerates what is already underway or about to begin.**
    This is a key distinction between coaching and other disciplines. Because our perspective is that the person is already whole and complete, we're not moving immediately into fix-it mode or bringing a scarcity mentality. Instead, we look for clues and dig for treasures in what we see in front of us. Coaches enjoy spending time at the intersection of curiosity and wonder.

    So many of the individuals and teams that I coach initially have little or no awareness of what is already underway or about to begin. One of the benefits of the coaching process is that it creates space in the coachee's schedule–even if it's only 30 minutes–to step back and see what is. Through deep listening and powerful questions, the coach helps the other person gain greater clarity about what they really want and also clarity about what God may be up to. Eugene Peterson, in his translation of Proverbs 29:18, captures the essence of this when he writes:

    "If people can't see what God is doing, they stumble all over the place. But, when they attend to the things of God (see what God is doing) they are most blessed..."

    Coaches help people see what God is already doing.

3. **Coaches maximize potential, moving people from good to great.**
   Coaches do more than inspire or cheer-on; coaches help people develop and actually make forward progress. Have you ever heard of a masterful athlete who achieved any success without coaching? A coach will develop you further, faster and deeper than you could ever do on your own.

One of the ways that we maximize in coaching is by tapping into the greatness of those we coach. Coaches intentionally look for and develop the strengths and giftedness of the person being coached. I appreciate the way in which Benjamin Zander explains this in his book, *The Art of Possibility*. Zander begins each term by informing his students that they already have an "A." Our coachees also begin with an "A." (We'll talk a little more about Ben Zander later in this book.)

One of the best illustrations of beginning with an "A" is the story of young David preparing to fight the giant Goliath. King Saul, who was tall and strong, put his own armor on David for the fight. (King Saul viewed David as lacking his own strength. Definitely not an "A".) Young, small David could barely stand up while wearing King Saul's armor. David took off the armor, picked up five smooth stones and killed Goliath. (1 Samuel 17:38-40)

David already had all he needed to fight the giant; he was already an "A." He just needed to tap into his strengths, gifts and God-given greatness. Coaches help people tap into what's already there and use it in their current situations.

Another way that coaches maximize potential is by looking beyond solutions to shifts. Shift work involves internal perspectives, beliefs and assumptions. I like to tell people that as a coach I "shine a flashlight" on their perspectives, beliefs and assumptions and help them see how these support and limit their forward progress. Let me give you an example. Many years ago I had a belief that I was "just a pastor" and that no one would hire a pastor as their coach. There were no external solutions or action plans that could adequately address this internal belief. Instead, my coach helped me create an awareness of how this internal belief was limiting me, plus he helped me gain an entirely new perspective on this belief.

Eventually, one day the shift happened and I saw the same thing completely differently. All of a sudden, I just knew that there were people who would want to hire me as their coach *because* I was a pastor. That was all that was needed. A giant leap forward followed.

Another way that coaches maximize the potential of coachees is to walk beside them, rather than trying to lead them. The coachee remains in the driver's seat, but the coach is invited along for the ride. I really like this expression: A coach is not a sage on the stage, but a guide alongside. How true! We fully help others develop their potential, but not by doing for them or telling them what to do. In this role of "guide alongside" the coach becomes:

- Your partner in achieving professional and personal goals.
- Your sounding board when making decisions.
- Your support in professional and personal development.
- Your guide in communication and life skills.
- Your motivation when strong actions are called for.
- Your unconditional supporter when you take a hit.

How is Coaching Different from Therapy, Consulting and Mentoring?

Let me first say that coaching is not the "be all and end all" of helping people. While there are tremendous benefits to coaching, the same is true of therapy, consulting and mentoring. All are of value. Taking that a step further, I believe that it is absolutely essential that we, as coaches, appreciate the important contributions that therapists, consultants and mentors make to the ongoing success of those we coach. In fact, about a third of those I coach are also using the services of a therapist, consultant or mentor.

During a break at a training event I was facilitating, there was a consultant in the group—obviously hot under the collar—who stated that because I was training all these people to be coaches, no one would need him anymore. My response to him was that I believed just the opposite: As the coaching industry grows, more and more individuals and organizations recognize that there are times when the expertise of a consultant, therapist or mentor is exactly what they need. I don't think he believed me.

Second, there is much overlap between coaching and therapy, consulting, and mentoring. Consultants identify with the brainstorming, designing the plan and follow-through elements of the coaching process, while mentors relate to our "guide alongside" philosophy. During a recent coach training event for therapists, a participant stated that many of the listening concepts and skills he was learning were very similar to what he learned as a therapist. Another marriage and family therapist defined coaching as "therapy for healthy people" and declared how refreshing it would be to work with people who were basically whole and complete.

Third, many coaches see the benefits of combining coaching with these other treatment modalities. A perfect example is the mentor-coaching that I offer coaches. Those I mentor-coach benefit from the access I have to both mentoring and coaching skills and techniques. Sometimes I blend the two; other times I use one or the other. There are also many consultants and therapists who now blend coaching into their practices. Note that it is very important to clearly understand the similarities and the differences when intentionally overlapping coaching with another discipline or skill set.

Fourth, coaching is still new enough that there are many competing perceptions about what it is. Someone who offers coaching may or may not be adhering to the techniques and approaches you are learning here. I once attended a coach training event where the trainer stated that when he works with his clients, "I just tell them what to do. That's what they are paying me for." That's definitely NOT how we define coaching around here!

Coaching Versus Therapy

Over the years, I have gathered several key distinctions between coaching and therapy. One distinction is that therapy is about recovery, while coaching is about discovery. For the most part, therapy is about recovering from a pain or dysfunction, often arising from the past. The focus is on recovering overall psychological health. Coaching, on the other hand, assumes an overall level of health and wellness and therefore isn't focused on recovery, but rather on discovery. The coaching process happens in an environment of curiosity and wonder as we seek peak performance in those we coach. Using a timeline, therapy is usually recovering from the past, bringing the person into a healthy present. Coaches begin in the healthy present and launch out to create and discover the future.

Another helpful distinction is archaeology versus architecture. Therapy, like archaeology, digs into the past to uncover hidden meanings that help us understand both the past and the present. Coaching, similar to architecture, builds on the solid, healthy foundation of the person as they are today, with the primary focus to design, create and support. I often remind new coaches that unless there is forward progress, or signs that forward progress is coming, it's not really coaching.

One more distinction: therapy versus therapeutic. Many individuals and groups report the therapeutic benefits of coaching; they generally feel more positive about themselves, as well as their present and future, as a result of coaching. Yes! It feels good to really make progress and actually accomplish what you set out to accomplish. Coaching is therapeutic, but it's not therapy. Those who coach have an ethical obligation to make referrals for therapy when needed. Indicators may include:

- An increase in overall sadness
- Difficulty focusing
- Changes in sleep patterns, appetite and anger
- Feelings of hopelessness
- An increase of risk-taking behavior
- Thoughts of suicide

Coaching Versus Consulting

There are two questions that come to my mind when I consider the distinction between coaching and consulting:

- Who is the recognized expert?
- Who is responsible for the outcome?

In consulting, the recognized expert is the consultant. Most people work with a consultant because they believe the consultant's expertise will benefit them or their organization. Usually the consultant helps diagnose problems and prescribes a set of solutions. In coaching, the recognized expert is the person or team being coached. The coaching perspective is that coachees are capable of generating their own solutions. The role of the coach is to provide a discovery-based framework that taps further into the expertise of the person being coached.

In fact, sometimes the biggest contribution I make to another person is three simple words: "I don't know." It is by being open to not knowing that allows a coach to propel the coachee forward.

As far as who is responsible for the outcome, in consulting, the consultant is responsible for the desired outcome. By following the consultant's advice, the client will achieve their desired outcome. Contrast this with coaching. Coaches seek to empower the one being coached. It is the coachee who is doing the work and is responsible for the outcome; they generate their own plans and take their own actions. The coach is responsible for holding the framework of the coaching process, but not for the outcome.

Coaching Versus Mentoring

Mentoring is a process of guiding another along a path that the mentor has already traveled. The sharing or guidance includes experiences and learning from the mentor's own experience. The underlying premise is that the insight and guidance of the mentor can accelerate the learning curve of the one being mentored. Although in many instances a coach and coachee might share a similar experience, it is not the coach's personal and professional experience that is of greatest value. In the coaching relationship, it is the coachee's experiences that are of most importance.

Does that mean that the coach never shares their experiences or expertise? Not at all. At a recent International Coach Federation conference, I learned that one of the things that coachees value most from their coach is when the coach shares advice and experience when asked for and when appropriate. Notice those qualifiers—when asked for and when appropriate.

When coachees come right out and ask me to tell them what to do, I usually preface any reply by saying something like, "Based on those that I have coached in a similar situation, here are a few ideas. What do you think?" In other words, I'm holding my advice lightly—remembering that it's my best-guess opinion and nothing more.

When is it appropriate to share our experiences and expertise? Sometimes the person we are coaching may be genuinely stuck, and offering advice may serve to prime the pump and get them thinking. Another time may be when a bigger goal can be met more quickly and effectively if they can leap over things of lesser importance. In all of these cases though, it is presumed that you have already established a coaching relationship of trust and safety, and you are both clear that this is only your opinion.

Initially, I recommend that new coaches refrain from offering advice. Most people have learned how to offer advice in ways that are not helpful and are, in fact, disempowering of others. First, we must learn how not to give advice. Then, we can begin to learn anew the art of advising. We'll talk more about this later in the book.

What Does a Typical Coaching Session Look Like?

In this hypothetical coaching scenario, a pastor stated,

"We're stuck! We've tried everything and nothing seems to work. We have the BIG picture… but can't seem to get started. The result is that we're losing momentum. It feels like we're taking one step forward and then two steps backwards. Leaders are bailing. I'm beginning to question my ability to lead. Help!"

A coach might employ one of these five strategies:

1. Ask the pastor to say more. One of the best places to begin is to simply invite the person to share further.

2. Mirror back what you're hearing and observing. It is amazing how helpful the simple act of mirroring can be. For the coachee, it is very beneficial to hear what they are saying and see how they are being heard.

3. Invite the pastor to describe the vision or BIG picture. In this scenario, the pastor states that "We have the BIG picture…but can't seem to get started." As the coach, I want to confirm that they really do have the BIG picture. Over and over again, I discover that leaders think that others have the BIG picture when they really don't. As a next step, I might encourage this pastor to facilitate more conversation about the vision. The group may have been too quick to move into strategy mode, and really needs to hang out a bit more with the vision.

4. Ask about the plan. This could very well be an implementation issue. It's not uncommon to develop a wonderful vision, hang it on the wall and assume it will just happen. A vision needs a plan. One of the top reasons a vision is never implemented is that it lacks a plan or the plan is poorly communicated.

5. Ask about their support system. Who can help them with this? In addition to a coach, other pastors and church members can be of tremendous assistance. There are numerous colleagues who have valuable insights and have learned from similar experiences. Tap into their experiences or seek them out as a sounding board and for an encouraging word.

What Do You Mean by a "Coaching Approach" to Ministry?

A growing number of today's spiritual leaders are pursuing coach training as a way of enhancing the mission and ministry of their own local church. Many are viewing coaching as a tangible way to address their role as "equipper." Ephesians 4:12 highlights the primary role of the spiritual leader as that of "preparing (equipping) God's people for works of service, so that the body of Christ may be built up." Coach training offers practical and proven tools and skills to equip God's people to build up the body of Christ.

One way to incorporate coaching into ministry is by coaching the groups and teams that we work with, instead of taking a more traditional leadership role. We can help these teams gain clarity about what they really, really want, then get out their way and let them make that happen. What is the result of this coaching approach to leading a team? You get a more effective team whose members are working from their strengths and greatness, rather than from their weaknesses.

When we supervise and evaluate others, imagine giving them an "A" before they even start. How much more empowering would that ministry setting be? Add to that the powerful questions we ask and the deep listening we offer and we have a recipe for success.

Our churches are filled with people experiencing personal, family, physical and spiritual transition and can greatly benefit from the coaching approach of support, clarity and accountability. Many spiritual leaders run small groups. Imagine if these groups were characterized by an environment of support and trust, led by group leaders who were skilled in bringing out the best in others. Personal transformation and life change are bound to follow.

Recently a new coach said to me that he believed that coaching was really a luxury for those in ministry, especially in this economy. My response: Effective leadership is not a luxury, but a necessity. Imagine the difference in you and your church if you partnered with a coach whose sole purpose was to bring out the very best in you and to help you to continually perform at that peak level. If our faith communities are going to be all that God intends them to be and if we are going to have the global impact we want to have, then coaching must not be seen as a luxury, but rather as a necessity.

THE FIVE STEP COACHING MODEL

Years ago, as a new coach, one of the most helpful tools for me was a coaching model. The following coaching model will provide you with a framework you can come back to over and over again as your coaching skills progress, and as you coach more diverse and interesting people and situations.

Solid coaching, like a solid house, has a:

- Foundation
  - Listen
  - Evoke

- Supportive Frame
  - Clarify
  - Brainstorm
- Strong Covering
  - Support

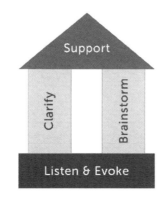

Laying the Foundation

Step 1: Listen

The goal as a coach is to listen so closely to your client that the answers come out. The ideal ratio is that you are listening 80% of the time and responding 20% of the time. It is absolutely critical that the client feels fully understood. Listen deeply by using these suggestions:

- Listen not just with your ears, but with your eyes and your whole being ("gut-level" listening).
- Listen to the tone, inflection, rate and pitch.
- Listen not just to what's said, but to what's not said.
- Pay particular attention to the last thing that is said.
- Listen without judgment, criticism or agenda.
- Listen without thinking about what you will be saying next.

Step 2: Evoke

Prompt the coachee to say more. Evoking is like opening the tap. You are attempting to get beyond the surface and move to the source of the issue.

Examples of evocative responses:

- Hmmmm.
- What else do you want to say about this?
- Tell me more.
- Is there anything else you want me to know?

Propping Up the Supports

Step 3: Clarify

Once the coachee has shared and has actively engaged with you, it's important to respond and clarify what is being said. This offers the client an opportunity to hear what they have just verbalized from a slightly different perspective. It also ensures that you and the client are on the same page.

Examples of clarifying techniques:

- I heard you say… (mirroring)
- I sense that… (paraphrasing or reflecting back)
- Is this what you mean? (verifying)
- On a scale of 1 to 10, how committed are you to this? 1=not important, 10=important (rating)
- Number these things based on which is most important to you. 1=least important, 10=most important (ranking)

Step 4: Brainstorm

Once there is clarity about the topic at hand, you and the coachee can now begin to go below the surface and further discuss the issue. Questions are central to the coaching process.

A few examples of questions include:

- What are the options/opportunities here? Let's list them all.
- What's the simplest solution? What's the craziest solution?
- What's the payoff of NOT dealing with this?
- What's stopping you?
- What do you want to be able to say about this situation three months from now that you can't say today?
- What do you really, REALLY want?

A more complete list of questions is found in the section about powerful questions later in this book.

Providing a Cover

Step 5: Support

Action is central to the coaching experience. Supporting the coachee to design an action step helps move the coachee forward, closing the gap between where they currently are and where they want to be.

A typical coaching conversation might end like this:

- Based on our conversation today, what action would you like to take? And when will it be completed?
- What do you want to report back to me at our next coaching session?
- What will bring you closer to your goal?
- What do you need to do in order to focus on this next week?
- What will get in the way?
- Who can help you with this?

In subsequent coaching sessions, you'll follow up by asking questions such as:

- What did you accomplish?
- What didn't you accomplish that you said you would?
- What got in the way?
- What's next?

INITIAL CONTACT WITH A NEW COACHEE

This section will cover your initial contact with a coachee or potential client in the role of coach. The areas covered include the complimentary coaching consultation and the welcome packet. In most cases, your initial contact will be a complimentary coaching consultation.

The Complimentary Coaching Consultation

The Complimentary Coaching session is generally a 45-50 minute session. The purpose of the complimentary session is to provide your potential coachee with an opportunity to experience you as a coach, plus for you as the coach to discern the potential "readiness" of the coachee for coaching. There are three sections to a typical complimentary coaching session. They include:

- **Introduction of coach and coaching (5-10 minutes):**

  Briefly introduce yourself to the prospective coachee and ask them to do the same.

  Thank them for the opportunity to coach them.

  Take a few moments to explain what coaching is, as well as what it is not.

  Inform the coachee that this is a safe space and that you will hold this conversation in confidence.

- **Complimentary coaching (30 minutes):**

  Treat this like a real coaching session.

  During the coaching session, develop a next step plan with the coachee and request that they check back with you in two weeks regarding their progress. Ask that they check back with you, even if they do not hire you as their coach. Explain to them that a key component to the coaching process is follow-through and accountability.

- **Discuss possible next steps (10 minutes):**

  If the coachee is "ready" for coaching and the relationship between the two of you is positive, talk with the coachee about next steps.

  Talk with them about the results and benefits of coaching.

  Share your usual fees, as well as typical next steps to begin a coaching relationship with you.

Remember, some will be ready to hire you right after the complimentary coaching session, some will not. It is not unusual for a prospective coachee to want time to think things through. Give them that time and space. Do not pressure them.

Remind the coachee that whether or not they hire you, you would like to receive a follow-up report from them as to their progress, or lack of progress, in two weeks.

Thank them for the opportunity to coach them and end the session.

Coaching Welcome Packet

The Welcome Packet is a set of documents that prepares the new coachee for the coaching experience. A sample Welcome Packet is in the Resource Section of this book. The Welcome Packet includes:

- **A Welcome Letter.** This is an introductory letter that a coach sends to a new client that provides the following information:

  - A warm welcome to coaching and a thank you for selecting you as their coach.
  - General information about you as the coach, as well as information on the coaching process.
  - A coaching agreement.
  - Ways for your coachee to prepare for each coaching session. (First Coaching Session Report + Focus Report.)
  - The Ethics and Professional Standards that you adhere to.
  - Contact information on the coachee.

- **The Coaching Agreement.** This is your contract with the coachee that covers all aspects of the coaching agreement. It is highly recommended that you have an attorney review your contract to ensure it is legally binding and accurate.

- **The Focus Report Form.** This is a form that is used by the coachee to prepare for the upcoming coaching session. Generally, the form is sent to the coach prior to each coaching session. Some make this a requirement while other coaches make it optional.

  Many coaches have a separate report form for the first coaching session. It often provides the coach with additional information helpful to the coach and the overall coaching process.

SETTING BOUNDARIES

What is a Boundary?

A Boundary is the space you provide between yourself and others—physically, emotionally and mentally.

Why are Healthy Boundaries Important?

- Provide space for you physically, emotionally and mentally.
- Set parameters for the coaching services that you will provide others.
- Provide for a clear sense of self.
- Define what you need from others.

- Provide parameters for what you will and will not do.
- Protect the coaching relationship between you and the coachee.

According to the article "Protecting Personal Boundaries" by Laurie Pawlik-Kienlen, personal boundaries are evident and effective when you know who you are, and treat yourself and others with respect. When you have healthy boundaries, you have a framework for approaching both situations and people.

Healthy boundaries allow you to:

- Get clear on "who you are" and "what you need."
- Provide self-respect.
- Provide accountability for your actions, without taking on the problems of others.
- Respond without guilt, fear and/or anger.
- Promote healthy relationships with those you coach.
- Reduce stress.
- Promote a greater sense of peace, joy and confidence in relationships with others.

How Do You Build Effective Boundaries?

To build effective boundaries you must have clarity around what you need, want, like/dislike, and desire for yourself and your future. The best time to set boundaries is "proactively" before a boundary has been violated versus "reactively" after your boundary has already been violated. Reactive boundary setting can cause a number of issues within a relationship, as expectations will need to be re-established or re-negotiated.

When you are building your boundaries, consider the following:

- Be honest with what you want and don't want.
- Determine how you will communicate your boundaries.
- Be willing to address and enforce "boundary breaking" with others.

How Do You Set Boundaries as a Coach?

Setting boundaries with those you coach can be done in several different ways. A few options are listed below:

- Discuss boundaries during the Initial Meeting.

- Include boundaries in your written coaching agreement.

- Spell out expectations in your welcome letter.

- Address boundaries during the coaching process.

Why is Boundary Setting Difficult?

Boundary setting can be difficult at times, especially for new coaches. The coaching process is often an intimate experience. As coaches, we experience the core of "who" an individual is and support that person's efforts in moving forward. Those we coach share with us their hopes and dreams for themselves and others. As a result, those we coach often may feel a "closeness" to us. As a coach, this "closeness" can be advantageous in the coaching process. It can also, in the absence of healthy boundaries, be very dangerous for both the coach and coachee. For this reason, it is important for coaches to set boundaries.

Coaches that have difficulty setting boundaries often:

- Lack healthy self respect.

- Have difficulty with confrontation and conflict management.

- Burn out more easily.

- Have issues of anger, frustrations and/or feelings of manipulation toward others/ those they are serving as a coach.

- May not be "present-oriented" due to boundary conflicts.

- Have issues with "pleasing others."

- Have difficulty being assertive.

Setting boundaries is a needed skill for coaches to be effective. In order to "stay clean" in our communication with those we coach and to not get caught up in their "stuff," coaches must be able to set and enforce effective boundaries. When communicating boundaries, it is important to be candid, clear and respectful regarding the expectations and boundaries in the coaching relationship. Many coaches use the CCR approach:

Be CANDID

Be CLEAR

Be RESPECTFUL

Strategies for Confidently Setting Boundaries

- **Have a Plan for "Boundary Breakers."** Plan in advance how you will address broken boundaries and how and when you will make exceptions.

  Tactfully discuss expectations going forward.

  When a boundary requires you to say "no," share the "why" behind the "no."

  When a boundary is broken, communicate what will happen next and discuss how to prevent this from happening in the future.

- **Lead by Example.** Have boundaries and use them! Think about those you know who are successful at setting, communicating and enforcing boundaries. Consider how they interact with others and stay true to their boundaries. If you want others to respect your boundaries, make sure you clearly communicate them and don't let others infringe on them. Lastly, respect others' boundaries as you want them to respect your boundaries.

- **Know Your Needs.** Know what you need and desire to be successful. Consider your relationships and your life — what do you need in order to be successful? Once you know what you need, then ask yourself what boundaries you need to put in place to support your success. Lastly, communicate those boundaries to those with whom you interact.

- **Proactively Set Boundaries.** Set boundaries "proactively" versus "reactively." Sharing your boundaries in a proactive manner is a better strategy than deciding in the middle of a heated situation you are no longer going to "take it." Don't put your relationships in jeopardy because you haven't done your homework!

How Do You Proactively Set Boundaries With Those You Serve as a Coach?

- **Respect Yourself.** Respect yourself enough to both set and enforce your personal and coaching boundaries. Remember that, to be at your best with those you coach, you need to implement and enforce your boundaries. If you cannot enforce your own boundaries, it will be difficult for you to coach others to be the best they can be.

- **Show Others How to Treat You.** How we allow others to treat us "trains" them on what we expect in terms of a relationship. When you don't speak up or inform others about your boundaries, you are confirming that their behavior is acceptable in terms of their interaction with you.

Helping Those You Coach Set Boundaries

During the coaching process, your coachee will begin to adopt new behaviors, new ways of thinking and have new experiences. An important next step is to review and, at times, reset their boundaries. As their coach:

- Notice how their new behaviors, thinking and experiences are impacting how they relate to others, as well as how others are interacting with them as they move forward toward their goals.
- Initiate a conversation around boundaries. When appropriate, share your observations regarding their current boundaries.

What are the Signs and Signals Indicating You Need to Coach on Boundaries?

- They do not respect your boundaries, as their coach.
- They are constantly stressed.
- They do not know their limits.
- They routinely do not speak up for what they want and need.
- They have difficulty articulating what they want and need.
- They have difficulty with accountability—both in terms of their own accountability and taking on others' accountability issues.
- They habitually sacrifice their needs and wants for the needs and wants of others.

Techniques to Help a Coachee Develop Stronger Boundaries

- **Needs/Wants Definition.** Ask the individual to define their needs and wants as they move forward toward their goals. Once their goals are defined, have them list their boundaries in relation to their needs and wants.
  - Ask the individual what they need to move forward toward their goals.
  - Based on the above question, ask them to define what boundaries they need to establish to move forward.
  - Ask the individual to define what support they will need to be successful in implementing and enforcing their boundaries.

- **Assertiveness Conversation.** Have a conversation discussing their ability to assertively enforce boundaries.

- **Challenge Your Client.** If you notice a pattern of not speaking up for their boundaries or allowing others to take advantage of them, consider having a discussion about communicating boundaries and self-respect.

- **Accountability**. Watch for patterns of deflecting personal accountability or taking on accountability for other people.
  - Ask the individual to define what they are accountable for in relation to their boundaries.
  - Ask the individual to define where their accountability begins and ends.
  - Discuss the pitfalls of being accountable for other people's actions, situations, etc.
  - Discuss the negative impacts of not being accountable for their actions.

- **Limits Discussion.** If the individual has difficulty setting limits for themselves or with others, have a discussion around the power of setting limits and respecting yourself enough to enforce those limits.

Chapter Two

The Eight Building Blocks of Coaching

One of my favorite sections in any bookstore is the "How to" section. It's amazing how many "How to" books there are, and they cover an endless array of topics. How to: build a deck, fix your car, knit, cook, find your perfect mate, etc.

This section is your coaching "How to." Over the next several pages, you will discover the core competencies and skills of coaching—we call them building blocks. These building blocks will provide a framework for your coaching.

1. DEEP LISTENING

All coaching begins with listening!

Don't read any further until you really, REALLY get this. It all begins with listening. Far too often we take listening for granted. How many times has someone tried to help you by offering you a solution without hearing what the problem was? They mean well, but they aren't really helpful. Years ago, I had a medical doctor who would listen to me describe my symptoms for about 13 seconds and then he would begin backing out the door, prescribing before I'd finished. I quickly learned the art of standing in the doorway.

So coaching begins with listening—deep listening. The quality of our listening has a direct bearing on the quality of our coaching. We can't draw out the best in another person, or tap into their greatness, if we haven't listened for it.

Listening is one of the greatest gifts that you can offer another person. Listening, in and of itself, provides tremendous benefits. Consider the following case study:

Nancy Kline provided an opportunity for every member of a senior management team to listen and be listened to. The result reported was a time savings of 62%. This translated into 2,304 manager hours per year. (*Time to Think: Listening to Ignite the Human Mind*, pg. 70).

Another case study, Luke 19:1-10:

In Luke 19:5 and 19:6, Jesus spent time alone with Zacchaeus. As a guest, Jesus would have spoken, as well as listened, to Zacchaeus. Based on the crowd's response to Jesus' actions

(Luke 19:7), it had been years since anyone had listened to Zacchaeus. The results were immediate and life-long. A changed life. (Luke 19:9)

What is listening? Listening is...

- Being curious about the other person.
- Quieting your own "mind chatter" so that you can be fully present with another person.
- Creating a safe space for someone to explore.
- Conveying value. You are important to me!
- Not about giving answers, but exploring possibilities.
- Reflecting back, like a mirror, what you experienced from the person.
- Really "getting" another person.

And note that there's a huge difference between hearing and listening:

- Hearing is an auditory process. Listening is an intentional process.
- Hearing is done with the ears. Listening involves all of the senses and the total being.
- Hearing includes words, details and information. Listening adds deeper layers.
- Hearing is to know about someone. Listening is being with someone.
- Listening is a skill to be developed.

Coaches listen so closely that the answers almost come out on their own. The ideal listening ratio is to be listening 80% of the time and responding 20% of the time. Someone once told me that words comprise about 7% of what we communicate. In other words, most of our communication does not involve words. Coaches know this. That's why coaches listen at multiple levels. A coach needs to:

- Listen to what the other person is saying, as well as what they are not saying.
- Listen from deep within (gut-level listening).
- Listen to "get" the other person.
- Listen without judgment, criticism or agenda. You are creating a safe space for the person to share.
- Listen without thinking about what you will be saying next.
- Listen for values, frustrations, motivation and needs.

- Listen for the greatness in the person you are coaching.
- Listen for limiting beliefs and false assumptions. What does this person really believe the outcome or future will be?
- Listen for shoulds, oughts and musts. They are frequent indicators of obligation and guilt versus what the person really wants.
- Listen for the obvious. What is the other person not seeing or not aware of?
- Listen for the tone, pace, volume, inflection and frequently used words. Also, notice when these change.
- Listen for the larger context.
- Listen attentively to the end of the statements. Remember the old faucets with well water? You needed to let them run awhile before you got the good water. The best words often flow out last as well!
- Listen to your reactions as you listen.

To be able to listen at multiple levels, a coach must quiet their mind of any mind chatter or internal conversations. They must create a physical environment that promotes deep listening, by attending to the space and pace of life and by managing their scheduling and calendar. Coaches grow to be comfortable with silence—resisting the urge to fill the space. When I was a new coach, a seasoned coach told me that deep listening is similar to standing in a pool. In order to see the bottom clearly, you must be still—absolutely still.

Pause for a moment and consider your own potential barriers to deep listening. What are some steps you can take to address these challenges?

Here are some exercises to improve your listening:

Mute the TV. Since most of what we communicate is non-verbal, why not mute the TV and have some fun trying to guess what's being communicated? To really test your ability, tape the TV show, watch it with the sound muted, and then watch it again with the sound playing.

Mirroring. Pair up with a partner, with each person taking a turn to talk and to listen. When you're the listener, do your best to listen as if you were a mirror. Reflect back what you heard. Then ask: Did I get that right? Did I hear you correctly?

Tape record a conversation. With the permission of the other person, tape a conversation in which you intentionally attempt to listen deeply. Right after the conversation, write down what your deep listening revealed. Then, go back and listen to the recording of the conversation. What more did you hear? What had you missed?

Practice selective listening. Decide that for the next week that you are going to be selective in your listening and really listen for one specific element. For example, you might choose to identify the values you hear underneath people's words. Or you might listen only for signs of frustration, or for signs of greatness. Over the course of the week, pay attention to that one selected area, training yourself to listen for this one item. Notice when you hear the item clearly—what circumstances made that possible in you and around you? What was going on in the times when it was challenging to hear the item?

Remember, great listeners hear with their:

- **Ears.** They listen to the spoken words, as well as tone, pace, pitch and inflection. They listen for the essence of what is being said.
- **Eyes.** Most of our communication is non-verbal. Great listeners notice the body language of the one speaking.
- **Full body and being.** Gifted listeners notice how they are receiving the message. They pay attention to what is happening inside of them as they listen.

2. POWERFUL QUESTIONING

On my recent travels to deliver a coach training program, I heard a statement on the radio that stopped me cold: History changed when a single question changed; when we stopped asking, "How do we get to the water?" and started asking, "How do we get the water to us?"

What a radical shift for us as human beings!

My thoughts went immediately to how this relates to us in ministry. How would our churches change if we were to change our questions?

For example, here are some of the questions you might be asking now:

1. How do we get "them" to come to us?
2. How much longer can we afford a full-time pastor?
3. How do we get people to fund our budget?

Boards and leaders literally spend hours on Question #1, but I think that if we changed that question, we could produce entirely different outcomes. What if we asked, "How can we go to them?" Or, we could ask, "How can we have a positive impact on our community-at-large?"

Question #2 suggests scarcity thinking—focusing on what's lacking instead of what's abundant. What if we ask, "What more can we do with the resources we have?" What if we look at, "How can we develop the people we have so they can make a bigger contribution and everyone wins?"

In Question #3, it sounds like we're trying to cajole or even manipulate people into doing something they don't really want to do. What if we ask, "What are people most excited about, and how can we give them the opportunity to support us while fulfilling their own interests and passions?" People are happy to invest time, energy and resources when it is also satisfying to them.

I invite you to listen for the questions that you and your church are asking. Are they limiting, like our examples above, or are they powerful? And what's the difference?

One of a coach's greatest tools is powerful questions. Powerful questions are usually open-ended, leaving room for contemplation and reflection, instead of being limited to yes or no or specific choices. Powerful questions promote the exploration of new possibilities and stimulate creativity. They place the individual or group in a place of responsibility. They empower individuals and groups to consider what is right for them.

Powerful questions open us to possibilities beyond the reality that's in front of us today, stretching us into the territory of our visions to ask, "What is God's invitation for us in this situation today?"

Limiting questions, on the other hand, might not be questions at all. They may only be thinly masking a statement of blame or obligation of guilt, e.g., "Why did you do it that way?"

Have you downloaded the new FREE e-book, *The E3-Church: Empowered, Effective and Entrepreneurial Leadership That Will Keep Your Church Alive*? Each chapter contains ten powerful questions that are guaranteed to shift your mind. For your copy of this e-book, go to www.coaching4clergy.com. Here are just a few samples:

- How could you make better use of the strengths of your church?
- What kind of leader would you be if you were driven by passion?
- What dream have you long since given up on?
- Which of your roles could someone else be doing, and probably better than you?
- What's the worst thing that could happen if you did less?

What makes a question powerful? Powerful questions are:

- **Directly connected to deep listening, enabling the coach to craft the most effective question.** Early on in my coaching I believed there was only one right question.

I would even equip myself with a long list of questions that I could scan while coaching. What I quickly discovered was that the most powerful questions were created in the moment and the power of the question was directly related to my ability to listen deeply.

- **Brief.** They get right to the point. It can be difficult to resist adding an explanation or another question, instead of just waiting for the person to respond.

- **Free of any hidden agenda.** They are not leading or suggestive. In the coaching profession we refer to leading questions as "que-ggestions." Powerful questions help the person or group being coached to move further along the path of discovery.

- **Usually open-ended, promoting further conversation.** For the most part, yes/no questions usually result in a yes/no response, which force an end to the conversation and enable either/or thinking. Powerful questions promote both/and thinking, opening up the coachee up to a fuller range of possibilities.

- **Clarifying.** They help clarify and slow down automatic responses and thinking. Coaching clients have told me time and time again that they appreciate how coaching creates the opportunity for them to step aside—push the pause button— and discern what they really want.

- **Perspective-shifting.** Powerful questions invite us to walk across to the other side of the room and look at the same thing from a different angle or perspective.

- **For the benefit of the one we are coaching.** Remember that the coach is not the expert, and does not have to figure anything out or come up with solutions. Therefore, our questions must be designed to help the coachee discover and develop their own perspective and wisdom about the situation.

Types of Powerful Questions

Questions that help the person gain perspective and understanding:

- What's the truth about this situation?
- Who do you remind yourself of?
- What keeps you up at night?
- Is there anything else that would be important for me to know?

Questions that evoke discovery:

- What do you really, really want?
- What's perfect about this?
- What is the gift in this?
- What additional information do you need?
- How much is this costing you?
- Who can help you with this?

Questions that promote clarity and learning:

- What if things are as bad as you say they are?
- Where are you sabotaging yourself?
- What's the cost of not changing?
- What's next?
- What's past this issue?

Questions that call for action:

- What's possible today?
- How soon can you resolve this?
- Who do you know that's going through this?
- What does success look like?
- What's the first step? When will you take this step?

The scriptures are a rich resource for powerful questions. For example, in Genesis 3:9, God asks the first powerful question of Adam and Eve saying, "Where are you?" Think about this. Why does an all-knowing God need to ask a question, when obviously God already knows the answer? Why then did God ask this question of Adam and Eve? The reason is just what we've been talking about: God asked Adam and Eve this powerful question for their own benefit, as well as for the benefit of the reader.

Here are some other powerful questions that God asks in the Old Testament:

- God asked Cain two questions in Genesis 4:6 and 4:9, "Why are you angry?" and "Where is Abel your brother?"
- God asks Moses, who is offering one excuse after another, "What is in your hand?" (Exodus 4:2)
- In the year that King Uzziah died, God asks, "Whom shall I send?" and "Who will go for us?" (Isaiah 6:8)

Likewise, the New Testament also contains many powerful questions. As you read through the books of Matthew, Mark, Luke and John, you discover that Jesus was masterful in his use of questions. My all-time favorite question that Jesus asked is found in John 5:6. Jesus sees the paralyzed man waiting for the waters of the pool of Bethsada to stir so that he could get in the healing waters first, and asks, "Do you want to get well?" What a great question! In the man's response, he blames others for not putting him into the pool. Jesus follows his powerful question with a direct statement, telling the man to get up and walk. And he does.

Here is a sample of other questions that Jesus asked:

- When the disciples were in a boat in a terrible storm, Jesus asked, "Why are you afraid?" (Matthew 8:26)
- He asked the disciples, when they were faced with feeding a crowd of over 5,000 people, "Where shall we buy bread for these people to eat?" (John 6:5)
- He asked the 12 Disciples, when many of his other followers were abandoning him because of His message, "You do not want to leave too, do you?" (John 6:67)
- He asked the Pharisees, "Why do you want to kill me?" (John 7:19)
- He asked the woman caught in adultery, "Where are your accusers? Has no one condemned you?" (John 8:10)
- After teaching the crowds about how much God cares for them, He asked them, "Why do you worry about what you will eat and what you will wear?" (Matthew 6:31)
- He asked the man who was born blind—the one that Jesus had healed of his blindness— "Do you believe in the Son of Man?" (John 9:35)
- When Peter made his claim that he would die for Jesus, Jesus asked, "Will you really lay down your life for me?" (John 13:38) And then, after his resurrection, Jesus asked him, "Do you love me?" (John 21:17)
- When Pilate asked Jesus, "Are you the king of the Jews?" Jesus replied with a question: "Is that your own idea, or did others talk to you about me?" (John 18:34)

At the beginning of this section on powerful questions, you read that history changed when a single question changed. And you've just read how our scriptures are filled with examples of how a single question dramatically changed lives. Questions are a powerful tool at our disposal. A powerful question, created out of deep listening, can change everything. Change the questions, change your church.

Below are exercises, strategies and examples to further develop your understanding and use of powerful questions:

Scenario #1: Your leadership team has been unable to take action on something decided months ago. Your team seems stuck on this issue. What powerful questions could you ask?

Scenario #2: You are designing a worship service and are looking for a specific response from the congregation. What powerful questions could you ask?

Scenario #3: You are meeting with a couple who is struggling with an issue in their relationship. They have a fairly healthy relationship but are stuck on this one issue. Each one is blaming the other, saying things like, "She doesn't understand me," and "He never talks to me." What powerful questions could you ask this couple?

Val's Top 10 Questions

1. On a scale of 1 to 10, how would you rate...?
2. What's the payoff of not taking action?
3. What's the truth about this situation?
4. What's your vision?
5. What's past this?
6. What keeps getting in the way?
7. What's the simplest solution?
8. Who can help you with this?
9. What do you think about when you're lost in thought?
10. What do you really, REALLY want?

Some people collect stamps, coins or spoons—I collect questions. I'm positively intrigued by questions. For more of my favorites, please see Appendix A at the end of the book.

Jump Start Your Next with Powerful Questions

A common complaint I hear from leaders is about poor discussion and input from team members: "How do we get people to share their ideas and comments at our meetings? We even send out the agenda ahead of time and no one seems prepared to discuss things."

Let me offer a simple change that often jumpstarts the discussion. Instead of creating an agenda with topics to discuss, develop a couple of questions from your original agenda that start people thinking. For example:

Original agenda:

1. Financial Update
2. Pastor's Report

3. Worship Team Items

4. Etc.

Revised agenda with questions:

1. What are some ways to encourage consistent giving over the summer months?

2. Who can help us discern the current state of our church and begin brainstorming God's unfolding vision for our church?

3. It's standing room only at our 9:00 a.m. and 11:00 a.m. services. What is our next step?

3. ARTFUL LANGUAGE

Many of us grew up hearing the statement, "Sticks and stones may break my bones, but words can never harm me." Nothing could be further from the truth!

Our words matter. Our language can provide a platform that propels someone closer to their hopes and dreams. At the same time, our language can reinforce doubts and limiting disbelief—dashing hopes and dreams. Think of language like a scalpel; in the hands of the skillful and altruistic, it can be invaluable, while in the hand of the reckless or malicious it can have **devastating or deadly effects.** Language is like the paint brush in a coach's hand; it is the playground for our meaningful work.

Let's check out four pieces of equipment on the coach's playground:

- Our actual words

- The matching of words

- Distinctions

- Acknowledgement

Our Actual Words

Ask yourself—how are my chosen words resonating with the other person? In coaching, we often refer to this as how something "lands." Are my actual words fostering a safe and inviting environment that encourages the other person to go deeper below the surface to the core issues? Or, is the other person so busy dodging and ducking the zingers I'm hurling at them that they can only say "ouch!"?

In our day-to-day conversations, words often contain assumptions, presuppositions, judgments, manipulation and suggestions. In coaching conversations, we intentionally choose words that are neutral, non-manipulative and free of any agenda. Our tone of voice is equally important. The same word with a different tone can be received entirely differently.

The Matching of Words and Language

Coaches notice the words and phrases of the other person. When appropriate, a coach will match their words and phrases with the person they are coaching and introduce new words or phrases. Coaches also pay attention to the pace and pattern of the other person's language. For example, when asked a question, introverts tend to process first and then talk, while extroverts tend to process by talking. The seasoned coach will sometimes match the other person to convey a feeling of acceptance; other times he or she will intentionally change up the pace and pattern to get the coachee's attention and make a point.

The coach is also listening for words that help the other person learn, describe their values and define their reality. These can be very useful in facilitating a shift. Often these are popular words or phrases from current or past culture. They can include TV, movies, music, metaphors, stories and quotes.

Examples of metaphors:

- The fruit doesn't fall far from the tree.
- Breaking the glass ceiling.
- Swimming in a sea of choices.
- Drinking from a fire-hose.
- Pulling yourself up by your bootstraps.
- It sounds like you're on a see-saw.
- It doesn't work to leap a 20-foot chasm in two 10-foot jumps. (American proverb)

Examples of stories:

- Joseph's story in the Old Testament. "You meant it for evil. God meant it for good."
- The Emperor's New Clothes and the importance of truth-telling.
- Forrest Gump's "Life is like a box of chocolates."
- Humpty-Dumpty's lesson, that some things in life can never be put back together again.

Examples of quotes:

- "And the day came when the risk to remain tight in a bud was more painful than the risk it took to blossom." — Anais Nin

- "It is a terrible thing to look over your shoulder when leading, and discover no one is there." —Franklin Delano Roosevelt
- "Most leaders don't need to learn what to do. They need to learn what to stop." —Peter Drucker

Examples from popular media culture include:

- The song, "Don't Worry, Be Happy."
- "You're fired!" from Donald Trump's TV show, "The Apprentice"
- The TV show, *Survivor*, and the phrase "getting kicked off the island."
- A place "where everybody knows your name," as revered in the theme song of the long-running TV show "Cheers."

Distinctions

Distinctions are two words or phrases that are close in meaning, yet convey subtle differences. Those subtle differences create a new awareness that is instrumental in propelling the individual forward.

Consider the following distinction and the subtle, yet huge, shift it creates:

Definition by obstacles versus definition by opportunities.

- To define yourself by obstacles means that you are defining who you are and the decisions you make based on the challenges that you are facing. A life defined by obstacles is reactive. It is moving away from someone or something.

- To define yourself by opportunities means that you define who you are and base your decisions on your opportunities. It's not that you're ignoring the obstacles, you've just decided to keep your sights on the bigger picture—your vision. It is moving toward someone or something and is usually proactive.

Additional distinctions:

- Perfection versus excellence
- Adding more versus adding value
- Living by default versus living by design
- Working hard versus producing results
- Either/or versus both/and
- Prioritizing what's on your schedule versus scheduling your priorities

- Doing powerfully effective things versus being powerfully effective
- Planning versus preparing

If you've read our free e-book, *The E3-Church: Empowered, Effective and Entrepreneurial Leadership That Will Keep Your Church Alive*, note that distinctions are a much more subtle version of the huge mind shifts I ask you to make in that book. Below are the six shifts that I invite you, as a leader in your church to make:

- From diagnosing to developing
- From doing to empowering
- From telling to exploring
- From mindlessness to mindfulness
- From excellence to effectiveness
- From professional to entrepreneur

Acknowledgment

Most people, when asked to create a list of their weaknesses and also a list of their strengths, find it easier to list their weaknesses. Why? Many people assume that "if I can just fix my weaknesses or if I could only correct what's wrong with me, eventually I will be great!"

Consider the following: The average person, on any given day, has 12,000 to 50,000 thoughts per day. By the age of eight, most of those thoughts are negative thoughts. (e.g., I'm not good enough. I can't do it. What's wrong with me?) Your church and, in fact, the entire world are made up of people who already speak to themselves with judgment and disapproval.

Acknowledgment creates an environment of acceptance and safety. When people feel safe and accepted, they are more likely to be curious and explore new things.

The scriptures contain one acknowledgement after another from God to us. Consider the following acknowledgements:

- So God created humankind in his image, in the image of God he created them; male and female he created them...and God saw all that he had made, and it was very good. (Genesis 1:27 and 31)

- For you created my inmost being; you knit me together in my mother's womb. I praise you because I am fearfully and wonderfully made; your works are wonderful, I know that full well. (Psalm 139:14)

- Jesus acknowledges Peter. In John 1:42, Jesus looks at Simon (known to us as Peter) and acknowledges him by saying, "You will be called Cephas," which, when translated, is Peter—the Rock. Long before anyone saw evidence of rock-likeness in Peter, Jesus acknowledged what was there. This acknowledgement was a major turning point in Peter's life. Yes, the transformation of Peter into "Cephas" was a rocky one, but it happened.

- There are different kinds of gifts, but the same spirit. There are different kinds of service, but the same Lord. There are different kinds of working, but the same God works in all of them in all men. (1 Corinthians 12:4-6)

The book, *Living Your Strengths*, includes a Hasidic tale that teaches the importance of acknowledging our strengths.

When he was an old man, Rabbi Zusya said, "In the coming world, they will not ask me: 'Why were you not Moses?' They will ask me: 'Why were you not Zusya?'" That is God's question to each of us as well. We are not expected to be who we are not. We are expected to be who we are. (*Living Your Strengths,* by Albert L.Winseman, Donald O. Clifton and Curt Liesveld, Page 10).

Ben Zander understands the importance of acknowledgment. In *The Art of Possibility*, a book he co-authored with his wife, he describes what he announces to every new class of students: "Each student in this class will get an 'A' for this course. However there is one requirement that you must fulfill to earn this grade: Sometime during the next two weeks, you must write me a letter dated next May, which begins with the words, 'Dear Mr. Zander, I got my "A" because...' And in this letter you are to tell, in as much detail as you can, the story of what will have happened to you by next May that is in line with this extraordinary grade." This practice acknowledges the greatness within people and invites them to live into that greatness.

Our God and our faith is about the giving of an "A." It makes sense then that our churches also be about giving an "A"—genuinely tapping into people's greatness. Imagine if the average church in a local community gained the reputation of giving "A's," instead of judgment. Or, if the focus in a church shifted from what they are not to who they are, as well as who they are becoming. See your church as a place that is regularly telling people that they are fearfully and wonderfully made. How different would our world be?

P.S. In Nancy Kline's book, *Time to Think* (pages 62-64), we read about how society teaches us that to be positive is to be naïve and vulnerable, whereas to be critical is to be informed, buttressed and sophisticated. Many people are taught that to be appreciated is a slippery slope toward gross immodesty. It is as if, when you hear something nice about yourself and don't reject it instantly, you will, presto, turn into an out-of-control egomaniac. This is ridiculous.

Actually, change takes place best in a large context of genuine praise, Kline asserts. Appreciation (what we are calling acknowledgement) is important, not because it feels good or is nice, but because it helps people to think for themselves on the cutting edge of an issue. We should aim for a 5:1 ratio of appreciation to criticism. Being appreciated increases your intelligence and helps you to think better.

4. ACTION AND ACCOUNTABILITY

When we began exploring action and accountability, a participant at a coach training event declared, "Finally, the good stuff!" When I asked what he meant, he said that everything we had discussed up until now, while helpful information, didn't really matter unless action happened. In many respects, he was right. One of the primary reasons that a person or a group decides to work with a coach is that they want to take action and reach their goals. Action and forward progress are indeed the good stuff.

There are three components to action and accountability: brainstorming, designing the action, and follow through.

It's really tempting at this point in the coaching process to jump right in and design an action plan. I want you to resist that urge and instead take a few more moments to brainstorm. Why am I suggesting this? Our coachee's tendency is going to be to take similar action steps as before, if not the same exact actions. The trouble is that those same action steps are going to generate the same outcomes. The reason this person or group is in coaching is to get different results! A quote on my office wall reminds me of this principle: Nothing changes, if nothing changes.

Brainstorming helps someone see the same thing differently. Brainstorming enables the individual to discover for themselves different perspectives and possibilities. This involves distinguishing between fact and perception/interpretation, as well as gaining clarity and defining success.

A great example of brainstorming occurred during an episode of the TV sitcom "Seinfeld," featuring Jerry's friend, George Costanza. George was one of those people who couldn't do anything right. He was in his 30s, he still lived at home, he had no job or relationship and was losing the rest of his hair. And he was often thought of as being unattractive.

And then George Costanza had a major epiphany. George said something like this: "Jerry, it's very clear to me that my life is the opposite of everything I want it to be. From now on I'm going to do the opposite."

Do you remember what happened when George did the opposite? Things turned out very well because George was willing to look at things entirely differently and step out of his comfort zone.

I want my coachees to have those kinds of epiphanies when we brainstorm together before creating an action plan. I usually start by asking them to identify a next step; what they would usually do next. Then, I ask them to set that action aside for the moment, and come up with 50 other possible actions. Most laugh at this request. Many are speechless. I re-state my request and give them some prompts, such as:

- What's the most outrageous step you could take?
- What's the simplest next step?
- Who could help you generate more ideas for next steps?
- What possibilities have you repeatedly dismissed?

Years ago I coached a pastor about casting the vision of his church. His usual method of vision-casting was to preach a rousing vision sermon the first Sunday of the New Year. Upon inquiry he acknowledged that this method stirred people for a couple of days, but produced no real progress. I then asked him to set that action step aside and I requested that over the next two weeks he identify 50 other ways to cast vision. He repeatedly stated that he didn't know any others. I repeatedly requested he come up with his list.

Two weeks later he came back with a list of 50 ways to catch the vision, and here's how he did it: The evening after our previous coaching session, he went to the praise team rehearsal and he kiddingly told the praise team about the outrageous request his coach had made of him—50 ways to cast our vision. The lead guitar player began playing the rock song "50 Ways to Leave Your Lover" and within minutes the vocalists began singing "50 Ways to Cast Our Vision." In the following moments, with the help of his praise team, he had his 50 ways to cast vision. Now he was ready to design the action plan!

Designing the Action by Creating a Plan

Within the context of brainstorming, a plan begins to emerge. The plan includes next steps that are attainable, measurable, specific and have target dates. In most cases the plan addresses both what you need to do and who you need to become in order to reach your goal. Commitment, like the "50 Ways to Cast our Vision," usually comes naturally and effortlessly.

Techniques useful for designing the action include:

- **Baby steps.** Sometimes people are immobilized with all that needs to happen. Breaking the action steps into smaller steps can help them begin taking action.
- **Backward planning.** Begin at the end (the goal) and then move backward and develop steps to get to the goal.
- **Acknowledging.** Recognizing what has been accomplished.
- **Creating structure.** Identifying what and who will keep the client focused on the task at hand.
- **Strategizing.** Considering what might derail progress and designing action steps in advance.
- **Anchoring.** Regularly reminding the person or group of the importance of what they are doing and where they are in the plan.
- **"Blitz Days."** Helping them carve out solid blocks of time to tackle everything that is getting in the way or needs to be done to stay on task.
- **Identify daily action.** These help create daily movement and momentum.

Sometimes formulas can be helpful. Consider the G.R.O.W. Model.

G	Goal	What's the goal?
R	(Current) Reality	How are we doing?
O	Opportunities	What are our current opportunities?
W	What	What's the next step?

Follow-Through

In an ongoing coaching relationship, there are built-in natural opportunities to check in regarding ongoing progress and to make course corrections. In most cases, I coach people twice a month—that's two times every month for us to follow through. I usually begin each coaching session with questions like these:

- What's happened since the last time we met?
- What didn't happen that you really intended to happen?
- What got in the way? What were the challenges?
- What will you report back to me the next time we meet, regarding this action?
- What do you want to focus on today?

Notice that the accountability is palatable as we define completion. There is no judgment or shame involved. There is no guilt or manipulation. This ongoing accountability is a natural part of the coaching relationship. A pastor once stated that accountability is really about "goaltending."

5. THE COACHING RELATIONSHIP

In real estate, the three most important things are: location, location and location. It can also be stated that, in coaching, the three most important things are: relating, relating and relating. The coaching relationship is the vehicle of change and transformation.

One way to view the coaching relationship is as a dance. Let's use the example of that great dance couple, Fred Astaire and Ginger Rogers, to describe the dance of the coaching relationship. Consider Fred Astaire as the coachee and Ginger Rogers the coach. Notice that Ginger did everything Fred did (only backwards and in high heels!), but that she takes her lead from Fred.

Let's stay with the dance of coaching to further understand the unique and skillful way in which a coach relates. Fred and Ginger developed a safety and trust that let them draw close to each other. A level of intimacy was present, yet never violated. This allowed them to really "get" each other and almost anticipate each other's moves. Coaches are able to be totally spontaneous, while also being fully present and in the moment. This total spontaneity involves a knowing that is beyond what is typically, or rationally, known and observed. It's similar to the athlete who can anticipate where the ball will be thrown, before it's thrown.

New coaches often ask me how to further develop coaching presence—a deeper level of knowing. There are no shortcuts to develop a deeper level of knowing. It all begins with deep listening. Practice listening, and then practice again and again. Develop and use powerful questions, and make artful choices with your language. Here are some additional tools that have helped others I've trained:

- **Note-taking.** The act of writing helps many go deeper. Jot down what you're noticing in the coaching session. Remember, deep listening uses the eyes, as well as the ears. The challenge of note-taking is to take notes in such a way that it enhances, rather than interferes with, your deep listening.
- **Self-care.** It's hard to go deeper when you're barely managing life on the surface. Go for extreme self-care. It's time!
- **Review your coaching.** Make a recording of a coaching session and then review it.

Then take it one step further and ask your mentor-coach to review it and give you feedback, specifically about your coaching presence.

- **Prayer and meditation.** Intentionally quiet yourself before and after a coaching session. How you show up matters.
- **Risk.** Share your hunches, inklings or gut feelings. Preface your hunch by saying something like, "I'd like to go out on a skinny branch for a moment with you, and I could be completely wrong, but here's what I'm wondering (or noticing)…"
- **Listen from the heart versus the head.** Be intentional in shifting from intellect to intuition. Request that the person you are coaching also get out of their head and listen from the heart. Ask them "What are you feeling in your body right now? What might your body be trying to tell you?"

Let's go back to Fred and Ginger for another unique component of the coaching relationship. Notice that Fred and Ginger aren't trying to correct or judge each other's steps while they dance. There is a mutual respect for the other's level of skills and competence. They each have their unique experience, strength and gifts. And the way that they relate to each other brings out the best in the other. On the dance floor they are tapped into each other's greatness.

How do you tap into the greatness of the other person or group? One resource to explore is my e-book, *The E3-Church: Empowered, Effective and Entrepreneurial Leadership That Will Keep Your Church Alive*, which has a chapter devoted to this shift from diagnosing to developing. In your day-to-day work and personal life, practice intentionally listening for greatness. At first you'll probably notice how much easier it is to diagnose, and how frequently you miss the greatness. Be kind to yourself—most of today's spiritual leaders, paid and unpaid, have been formally and informally trained to diagnose problems. Over time you'll begin to notice greatness more readily.

Next, begin to tell others about the greatness that you observe in them. They may dismiss it or disqualify it. Keep telling them anyway, because what's important is the shift you're making in how you relate to them—as a whole and complete person or team. Eventually, like Ginger and Fred, you'll be tapping into the greatness of others with ease and grace. And you'll also notice that your new way of relating will be an attractive magnet for drawing people to you and your coaching.

The complimentary coaching session is an ideal opportunity for a coach and a prospective coachee to discern whether you relate to each other well enough to develop a powerful coaching relationship. A positive coaching relationship will increase your coachee's likelihood of success. Since they relate well to you, they are more likely to explore further and take bigger steps, plus they will stick with their plan of action longer.

6. THE COACHING AGREEMENT

As a pastor, I would often find myself needing to say, "If you need something from me, please tell me. If I don't know what you need or want, I can only guess at what you need and want. And I am not a mind reader."

The same is true of coaches—we aren't mind readers, and that's why we have a coaching agreement. A coaching agreement is a way to define the requirements and process behind the coaching relationship. The coaching agreement takes most of the guesswork out of coaching and makes it possible for the coach to follow the coachee—not the other way around.

While newer coaches see the coaching agreement as a once-and-done process, masterful coaches understand the ongoing nature of the coaching agreement and that there are three parts to the coaching agreement:

- The initial agreement
- The ongoing agreement
- The evaluation process

The initial coaching agreement includes:

- Defining the terms of the coaching relationship in writing; for example, fees, schedule, responsibilities, and expectations of the coach and coachee.
- Articulating what coaching is and isn't.
- Discerning whether or not the coach and coachee are a good match.
- Clarifying the needs of the coachee and why they want to work with a coach. I like to ask, "What do you want to be able to say three months from now that you cannot say today?" This helps both the coach and coachee gain clarity about the desired outcome.

The ongoing coaching agreement includes:

1. Helping the coachee clarify what they want to focus on in each particular coaching session, as well as what they want to take away.
2. Further clarifying and exploring what the client is taking away from the coaching session.
3. Holding side-by-side the initial desired outcomes and goals that brought them to coaching and the current focus/take-away. Because coaching is focused on discovery

and not outcomes, new insights and perspectives need to be continually integrated into the coaching agreement.

The third component of the coaching agreement is the evaluation process. This frequently includes course corrections, or may also involve a dramatic shift in the overall desired outcome. I frequently ask questions, such as:

- How are we doing?
- Based on our coaching to date, what's your ongoing, developing vision?
- On a scale of 1-10, rate the overall progress you've made. What is needed to take it up several levels?
- What more do I need to know about you, your learning preferences or background to accelerate your progress?
- Where is self-sabotage showing up? What additional support is needed?
- What will you report back to me the next time we meet?

A frequent mistake that new coaches make is in moving through the coaching agreement quickly—in as little as two to five minutes. I've discovered that the clearer the coachee and coach are with the agreement, the better the outcome. It's not unusual for me to spend the bulk of a coaching session on this area—15-20 minutes. Here are questions and statements that help my coachee and me to fine-tune our coaching agreement and evaluate the coaching process:

- Tell me more. Because people are so busy, they rarely have time to think and talk. It's extremely beneficial to intentionally provide space for people to say more. Time and time again I hear coachees extol the benefits of "getting things out."
- What is the one thing I need to hear in order to best coach you? This helps the coachee get laser-focused and selective about sharing only what's absolutely critical to their overall progress.
- Taking into account all that's on your plate right now, is this topic/issue the most important one (and if not, what is)? Similarly, this question helps the coachee hone in on the topics and issues that will contribute the most to their overall success and satisfaction.

This coaching scenario will help you to further understand the coaching agreement:

> Steve is the founder and Senior Pastor of a rapidly growing church. He currently has 22 full-time employees on his ministry team. He frequently describes his team as a family. It's not unusual for Steve to "go the extra mile" and bend the rules

for individual members of his team, because he considers them to be his family. He finds it difficult to fire even the worst of the ministry staff, because he's really concerned about their welfare.

Steve's vision is to grow from a single site to a multi-site ministry. He believes that he can do this within the next three to five years. In addition to implementing this multi-site vision, he would also like to spend less time at church and enjoy life more. His big dream is to take the whole year off and let the ministry run without him.

Steve has created a strategic plan and action steps to move towards his goal. He's making moderate progress. He is becoming very aware that his current ministry team is slowing things down. He is also frustrated that his "ministry family" doesn't share his enthusiasm for his vision. Steve initially hired a coach to help him implement the multi-site ministry plan, with a special emphasis on how he can empower and equip the ministry team to lead the implementation plan.

During a recent coaching session, Steve expressed frustration about his vision and his "ministry family" and then made the following statement about himself, "Maybe I'm the one that's holding back this vision. It feels like all the pieces are there, but maybe there's something that needs to change about me."

In your words, describe the focus of this coaching relationship (as may have been determined in the initial coaching agreement).

What are Steve's new discoveries? What other new discoveries do you see ahead for Steve?

In what ways will these new discoveries impact the coaching agreement?

In what ways will the coaching agreement remain the same?

After hearing Steve state, "Maybe I'm the one that's holding us back," how would you coach Steve?

7. CREATING NEW AWARENESS

Brainstorming is an excellent way to explore new ways of doing things. Creating awareness takes it one step further and explores new ways of being, as well as doing. It's like working the plates deep within the earth, resulting in major shifts and changes. Let me give you several examples:

- Consider this statement from one pastor I coached: "I'm an introvert and everyone knows that introverts aren't good leaders." No amount of doing would result in any lasting change. This pastor needed to go down deep and create a new awareness of his strengths.

- Consider the leadership team that fizzled out partway through a visioning process. The consultant tried everything to get them moving, and then finally inquired what was happening. After what seemed like an eternity of silence, one of the key leaders finally responded that they had gotten to this point on two previous occasions within the past five years and, in each instance, their pastor had moved on before the projects were completed. No sooner had the words been spoken when the leadership team had a major "a-ha." They embraced their new awareness and began moving forward.

- Consider the awareness that launched my career as a full-time coach. As a part-time coach, my business growth was slowed by the belief that I was just a pastor and no one would hire a pastor as their coach. When my coach helped me verbalize this limiting belief, it created an awareness of the truth that my ideal clients will seek me out and hire me precisely *because* I am a pastor.

Creating new awareness is like raising the blinds and letting in the light of additional information, perspective and intention. New awareness is fostered when:

- Curiosity is encouraged.
- Clarifying questions are raised.
- Beliefs and assumptions are articulated and verified.
- You intentionally consider a different perspective.
- You are open to other ways of viewing and interpreting the same situation.

How does the coach facilitate new awareness?

- Contextual listening. The coach considers and explores the various contexts of the person being coached (e.g., the bigger picture, the total person, previous experiences, and the values of the person). When David pulled out his slingshot to fight Goliath, he was drawing on earlier contexts of time when he had fought wild animals with his slingshot.

- Missing pieces. The coach helps individuals and groups see and say what they can't quite see or say. Because the coach is listening on multiple levels, the coach hears underlying values, motivation, greatness, frustration, etc. Simply being a mirror and holding up for the other what we're observing creates new awareness.

- Drilling down. Similar to the layers of an onion, the coaching process peels away the layers and gets to the core issues.

- Listening for clues. A coachee is always offering clues about themselves. R.D. Lang wrote, "The range of what we think and do is limited by what we fail to notice. And because we fail to notice that we fail to notice, there is little we can do to change; until we notice how failing to notice shapes our thoughts and deed." Here are some powerful questions that will uncover important clues:

  - What kind of problems and crises do you keep attracting?
  - What do you keep doing that limits your success?
  - What thoughts are repeatedly playing in your head?

Eliminating Limiting Beliefs and False Assumptions

One of the most powerful ways of creating awareness in a coaching relationship is to help the coachee identify and transform their limiting beliefs and false assumptions.

Use the following list to see if you recognize some of your own:

- I have to have all the answers.
- I have no choice. I have no power.
- I cannot lead.
- Change is always difficult.
- It isn't possible.
- What doesn't kill you makes you stronger.
- Peace is always better than honesty.

[handwritten notes in right margin:]
Five "S" Coaching Model
Symptom
Situation
Source - where is this coming from?
Solution
Shift - what internal reorientation needs to happen

List three of your limiting beliefs:

1. _____
2. _____
3. _____

List three of your false assumptions:

1. _____
2. _____
3. _____

Limiting beliefs and false assumptions can be very simple, yet very harmful. In her book *Time to Think,* Nancy Kline offers a simple yet profound method of dealing with limiting beliefs and false assumptions. One of her tips is to help your coachee articulate the "positive opposite" of their limiting belief or false assumption. This is often a difficult task for an individual or team to do, but press them to articulate the positive opposite of their bedrock assumption. Once articulated, ask them to write it down and say it several times.

8. DIRECT COMMUNICATION

If you spend time with a seasoned coach, you will notice the masterful way that they communicate. For example, you will almost never hear a masterful coach ramble. Most seasoned coaches are clear, concise and laser-like with their words, offering one question or statement at a time.

Another characteristic is their comfort with silence. There is no attempt to idly fill space; rather, an appropriate use of silence and pauses is demonstrated. And coaches tell the truth. They don't hold back on whatever needs to be said, even if that isn't always the nicest thing to hear or the most comfortable thing to say.

Seasoned coaches are direct in their communication, using language that will have the greatest positive impact on the person being coached.

Four of the most important direct communication techniques are:

- Interrupting –
- Advising — *After Learning all facts / lightly*
- Directing — *Hold that thought - Let's Talk about it. / Congrats - Let's move on, etc.*
- Messaging

Interrupting — *Let person know you may 'interrupt ahead of time*

Most of us have experienced interruptions that are distracting or annoying, but effective interrupting is truly an art. As a coaching skill, masterful interrupting holds great benefit for the coachee, bringing them back on task, or helping them to "bottom-line" (get to the point).

Coaches interrupt within an environment of trust and intimacy, in which the coachee trusts the skill of the coach and knows that the coach has their best interest in mind. Interrupting can stem from deep listening, as a means of getting at something even deeper that needs to be said. Interrupting is a platform from which to catapult the coachee forward.

During my initial coaching sessions with new coachees, part of our initial agreement is for them to give me permission to interrupt them—when appropriate. Having this conversation on the front-end of the coaching experience helps the coachee to expect the interruptions and see it in a positive light.

When is it appropriate to interrupt someone you are coaching?

Here are several ways that I may interrupt someone while coaching:

- Say their name and ask for permission, e.g., "(Name), may I interrupt you?"
- Break in with, "Let's push the pause button for a moment," or "I'd like to step in for a moment."
- Bottom-line it for them, e.g., "(Name), here's what I'm hearing..."

Advising

One of the myths of coaching is that coaches never give advice. That's a myth? Let me explain. First and foremost, the coach wants to tap into the expertise of the one they are coaching. Got it! And, there are also times when the coach has expertise and experiences that can have a positive impact on the forward progress of the coachee. During a workshop at an International Coach Federation conference, the presenter stated that #7 on the top 10 list of what people want in a coach is advice. The qualifiers are that they want advice from their coach when appropriate and when asked for.

The problem with giving advice is that most people offer advice in ways that are disempowering of others. They need to unlearn how to give *advice* and then re-learn how to *advise*. I suggest that newer coaches completely refrain from offering advice, at least for a time. Once they have learned how to effectively coach without giving advice, they can begin incorporating advice-giving into their coaching when appropriate and when asked for.

Consider the following tips when offering advice:

- Listen deeply. Hear all that the person has to say.
- Don't offer advice until you have thought through how the advice may be misheard.
- Don't give advice until you have heard all the facts.
- Don't forget that it's ONLY ADVICE; it's not a cure for global warming.
- Phrasing examples:
  - Here's what I've seen work. Tell me if it sounds like it's worth experimenting with.

    – That's a tough one. Here's what I advised another person and this is what happened.

Directing

Directing is a technique for re-focusing or steering the person or group back toward their goals. This is useful for the coachee who frequently goes off on tangents or easily loses sight of the big picture.

Examples of directing:

- Hold that thought and let's talk about...
- For the past several weeks we've been focusing on ABC, is it time to move on to XYZ?
- Congratulations. Let's move on.

Messaging

Messaging is a "truth" that, if heard, will help the other person to understand and act more quickly. It is a "blending" of acknowledging and tapping into the person's greatness.

Examples of messaging include:

- Tell them who they are. "You are someone who is . . ."
- Endorse what they have accomplished. "Wow. Look what you've accomplished. Congratulations."
- Tell them what's next. "You probably need to start focusing on ABC, because you've moved past XYZ."
- Tell them what you want for them. "What I want for you is . . ."

Chapter Three

Common Coaching Scenarios in Ministry

Common Coaching Scenarios in Ministry is designed to provide you with a basic understanding of nine common coaching situations experienced as a coach in a ministry setting. While our coaching of each person or group is unique, there are common themes and approaches that provide the coach with a framework from which to craft a coach approach to ministry.

A Few General Comments About This Resource Material

The purpose of this module is not to pigeonhole those you coach or to put them in a "one-size-fits-all" category. Our purpose is to provide you with useful tools and insights for coaching those in various ministry settings.

This material is intended to be a resource guide to help you identify and understand the common needs and outcomes of those in various ministry settings.

This material will assist you to identify and facilitate significant shifts in ministry.

The information contained in this module represents the collective knowledge, wisdom and experience of Coaching4Clergy coaches, who have coached extensively in these nine areas of ministry.

The nine common coaching scenarios we will address include:

1. Coaching the First Time Pastor
2. Coaching New Beginnings
3. Coaching the Lead Pastor
4. Coaching the Supervisor of Paid Staff
5. Coaching the Transitional (Interim) Pastor
6. Coaching the Executive Pastor
7. Coaching the Minister of Music
8. Coaching Those in Career Transition
9. Pre-marital and Marriage Coaching

1. Coaching the First Time Pastor

A Brief Description of this Situation

New pastors have the challenge of setting the foundation of their ministry, casting a vision, developing strategy, developing organizational capacity, training leaders and putting into place healthy boundaries of self care.

Typical Coaching Scenarios

- Pastor Gwen has taken her first pastorate. She is in a very traditional congregation. She knows it is important to observe traditions, but she does not want to just go through the drill enacting the same things each week without seeing people grow in their faith and impacting their community. She really needs a well-defined vision to guide her ministry.

- Pastor Gregg knows that to build a successful church they will need leaders. The pastor before him never developed the leaders around him and their meetings were more like business meetings focused around getting tasks completed. Pastor Gregg wants to help those around him to discover and cultivate their gifts and passions in ministry, and then deploy them in the position that optimizes both their talents and the needs of the church. Pastor Gregg would like to create or find a model for leadership development at all levels of the church.

- Pastor Steve is new in ministry and has inherited a church secretary and youth pastor. The secretary is not very efficient and tends to treat the job like a hobby often coming in late and leaving early. Although there are not many teenagers in the congregation, the previous pastor hired a youth pastor in the hopes of making the church more attractive to families with teenagers. Pastor Steve realizes that a strategy for appropriate staff, as well as strategies on how to deal with the current staff, would be beneficial.

- Pastor Sue has heard that many pastors burn out from too many ministry activities. She has also heard that many become 'professional' ministers, always looking at the Bible for sermon ideas, while they ignore the needs of their own hearts. She wants to be sure that her ministry is an overflow of her relationship with Christ and is always keeping her spiritual life fresh. Pastor Sue has a desire for strategies for devotional times, retreats and Sabbaths.

Common Outcomes and Shifts Indicated or Desired

The desire is for the new pastor to be set up for success. The common areas that a coach may help new pastors with are personal self care, assessing the existing situations, developing a clear vision, transitioning into a position while the church is transitioning along with them, setting priorities, and time management. Helping new pastors by creating awareness of issues and helping them develop wise and healthy boundaries is very beneficial.

• Attachment to own ideas—Observing and incorporating other's ideas
• Planning—Preparing
• Having or getting a staff—Develops / empowers others to do their part
• Self sacrifice—Godly self care

Best Practices: Coaching Skills and Strategies

Coach the pastor around a vision and ministry philosophy. Lack of these can contribute to the ministry digressing into 'doing the drill' on Sunday and not much more.

Coach the pastor to think through what kind of staff they need to accomplish their vision. It may not mean traditional staff hires like youth pastor or worship pastor, but outreach pastor or coaching pastor.

Coach the pastor to develop a healthy ebb and flow of ministry, allowing for intense periods of engagement followed by time of retreat and reflections. Jesus modeled this with His disciples.

2. Coaching New Beginnings

A Brief Description of This Situation

This section considers the dynamics that occur within the first 18 months of a pastoral transition, whether it is the pastor's very first church or the fifth.

Typical Coaching Scenarios

• Termination emotions that affect the new pastor, the clergy family and the parish.
• Coping with the stress of transition.
• Making entry into the life of the new congregation.
• Making changes.

- Assessing leadership styles and gaining role clarity.
- Developing a plan of ministry.

Common Outcomes and Shifts Indicated or Desired

To help pastors:

- Get in touch with their emotions, the emotions of their family and new parish.
- Implement self-care coping strategies.
- Identify their typical leadership style, the leadership expectations of the congregation and how far both are will to move.
- Identify strengths vs. self-defeating behavior.
- Move from role ambiguity, confusion and overload to role clarity.
- Develop a support system that addresses survival, stability and prodding.

Best Practices: Coaching Skills and Strategies

- Strengths-Based Coaching
- Coaching on Boundaries
- Vision Development and Strategic Planning Coaching
- Stress Management Coaching
- A Ministry Dashboard
- Personal Foundations

Additional Resources

A New Beginning for Pastors and Congregations: Building an Excellent Match Upon Your Shared Strengths, by Kennon L. Callahan

Ten Commandments for Pastors New to a Congregation, by Lawrence W. Farris

New Beginnings: A Pastorate Start Up Workbook, by Roy M. Oswald

Beginning Ministry Together: The Alban Handbook for Clergy Transition, by Roy Oswald, James M. Heath and Ann Heath.

Pastoral Transitions: From Endings to New Beginnings, by William Bud Phillips

3. Coaching the Lead Pastor

A Brief Description of This Situation

Lead pastors of small churches have the challenge of fewer resources and few or no staff. They tend to be overstretched, have boundary issues, and are frustrated with the lack of time that congregants give to the church ministry. They usually lack people qualified to be elders and ministry leaders.

Lead pastors of medium and larger churches typically face challenges in the areas of growth, economic realities and changes in staff. Implementing changes to better accomplish the ministry at hand and the business that supports it are frequent concerns.

Typical Coaching Scenarios

- Pastor Doug has a church of 200 but it is an aging congregation. He would like to make the church more family friendly. He has been showing some videos to his leaders and Sunday school classes on becoming a more relevant missional church and there has only been lukewarm response. Several of the older church members seem dead-set against any change. Pastor Doug fears that without the changes, in a few years the church will shrink and no longer be viable.

- Pastor Anne has a small but growing congregation. She left a lucrative career in the corporate world, went to seminary and has become a pastor. She has discovered that there is not the same accountability level as in the corporate world, as people often make promises and then do not follow through. She feels pulled in a hundred directions with all the differing demands of church leadership. Seminary gave her Greek, Hebrew and church history but no preparation on how to run a church. She is frustrated, exhausted and ready to quit.

- Pastor Craig just took over from the church's beloved pastor of 30 years. The first six months went well. Then everything started to fall apart. It started over Pastor Craig's simple plan to merge the choir and the contemporary worship teams under one leader. Several choir members spread rumors that the new pastor was trying to destroy the choir. Over the next few weeks, the choir director resigned, along with over half of the choir, and left the church. Meanwhile long time members of the church where not sure where the new pastor stood on many doctrinal issues and demanded that he write position papers on a number of issues to clarify his position. Over the next few weeks almost one third of the congregation left the church. Attendance and giving dropped off. While many church members voiced support for Pastor Craig, it was clear that many remaining had seen close friends leave and were also on the fence.

Common Outcomes and Shifts Indicated or Desired

- Pastors of growing congregations are often overwhelmed by the administrative demands. Small churches are often run as Mom-and-Pop shops with the pastor's family members filling major responsibilities that they often are not well trained for. There comes a point where the administrative model must move from a Mom-and-Pop to a more corporate or, at least, small/medium business model. Roles are best filled by people with the proper qualifications. Also, evaluation procedures must be put into place and underperforming leaders moved into other positions or let go. It is often difficult for a pastor to make this shift. If they don't, the size of the church will shrink down to match the level of administration.

- Pastors facing church splits are often in crisis. It is difficult for them to see clearly so many emotions are involved. Coach the pastor to fight the right battles. Going around answering every challenge and question is not helpful. Coach pastors to take the reins and define their ministry vision and begin moving forward. It is an opportunity to put their stamp on a new ministry.

- When coaching for congregational change, keep in mind that not everyone in the church needs to be on board for change to begin. Coach them around involving people, hearing their fears and discussing with them several steps that would be acceptable. Then, run with the small group that is ready to go and has been waiting and wanting change. As this group gets early wins in their efforts, highlight them to encourage more positive change. Also, don't be surprised if some congregants either stage a coup or leave the church, loudly voicing their displeasure on the way out. Letting go of the idea that everyone needs to be on board with proposed changes is often a catalyst for forward movement and growth. It can create a Win-Win for the Church and for those not in favor of the proposed change.

Best Practices: Coaching Skills and Strategies

- Coach pastors to clarify their vision and make sure that the changes they are proposing are not just to change things, but meant to promote the vision.

- Coach pastors to identify people who are ready to go and dream and strategize with them on some appropriate next steps to gain early wins. They may have a large vision but start with small, achievable objectives to build momentum.

- Coach pastors on having regular intervals of rest and retreat, as Jesus did with his disciples.

- Coach pastors through a process to define what they are most gifted at and what only they can do in the church, and begin to coach around how to communicate, train, delegate and empower others to take on the other tasks.

- Coach pastors about making only a few position statements that they deem necessary and allow the matter to drop. Create awareness about the cost of endless debate over religious issues and the benefits of highlighting what matters most.

4. Coaching the Supervisor of Paid Staff

A Brief Description of This Situation

The supervisor is responsible for his/her contributions and the contributions of his/her staff. In the end, the supervisor is typically responsible for the path and the outcome. Supervisor styles vary in how involved they are in the details of the path. The supervisor frequently seeks coaching to help determine the most overall effective way to get things done. The supervisor may also be called on to be a leader and inspirer. Coaching the supervisor of paid staff will help the supervisor draw out his/her own strengths to enroll, equip and enable the staff.

Typical Coaching Scenarios

- Supervisor has responsibility for implementing the vision, but is not seeing progress or alignment.
- Supervisor is dealing with budget cuts.
- Supervisor continues to experience problems with a staff member who has not been meeting the needs of the position.
- Supervisor and/or staff is stressed, overloaded or has multiple areas of responsibility to balance.
- Supervisor wants staff to take more responsibility.

Common Outcomes and Shifts Indicated or Desired

- Diagnosing—Developing
- Telling—Exploring
- Doing—Empowering

- Busy—Effective
- Knowledge—Wisdom
- Purpose—Courage

Best Practices: Coaching Skills and Strategies

Coaching Skills

- Acknowledge and recognize achievements of the supervisor.

- Anchor with reminders of who and where they are, then explore what they are doing. Focus on the vision and the "who."

- Actively listen, ask powerful questions and use direct communication around limiting beliefs, false assumptions, motivations, concerns and successes. Be sensitive in the moment for the amount of subtleness or boldness needed.

- Create awareness and use direct communication around the many different factors/ systems that affect the supervisor and staff member, such as marathon effect, generational and relationship patterns.

- Strategize for both the big picture and for work with individual staff members.

Coaching Strategies

- Systems Coaching—Awareness of the People Factor—Building transitions by coaching in these stages of change to recognize and address:
    - Ending of old way; hearing losses associated with the ending and getting ready to move on.
    - Seeing new possibilities and need to realign and form new patterns; searching and adapting.
    - Embracing new way and discovering new sense of doing things; aligning.
    - Recognizing marathon effect, the difference in timing of the above stages for head leadership, staff and congregation.
- Strengths Coaching—Identify strengths of supervisor and create awareness of strengths of supervisor's staff. Work from strengths.
- The Who—Look for common challenges in the supervisor's role and address the "Who."
- SMART Goals—Help the supervisor to ensure staff is equipped and empowered to succeed.
- Specific, Measurable, Attainable, Relevant, Trackable

Additional Resources

Marathon Effect, article by J. Val Hastings

Managing Transitions, by William Bridges

Executive Coaching with Backbone and Heart: A Systems Approach to Engaging Leaders with their Challenges, by Mary Beth O'Neill

5. Coaching the Transitional (Interim) Pastor

A Brief Description of This Situation

This section explores coaching at various stages of the interim journey[1] and during the developmental tasks set before the transitional pastor. Also covered are the characteristics frequently encountered in an interim congregation.

Typical Coaching Scenarios

- Feelings of grief the congregation will experience at the loss of their former pastor, which are often masked by feelings of disappointment, anger at abandonment, and a reluctance to make any changes, to name a few.

- Conflict that may be latent or active with the life of the congregation.

- Secrets that may come to light as seen in hidden agendas or serious issues of the past which have not been resolved.

- Lagging stewardship of money, worship attendance and volunteerism, particularly if conflict and disillusionment have set in.

- The former pastor's inability to set clear boundaries and accept he/she is no longer the pastor `

---

[1] Congregations experience eight stages in the interim journey:

1. Termination: Departure of the incumbent pastor
2. Direction finding: Learning about the steps to be taken before a new pastor will be called.
3. Self-Study: Congregation looks at itself, gathers data and prepares a parish description to share with prospective candidates.
4. Search: Congregation clearly focuses its identity and puts a search committee in place who will study candidate profiles and interview candidates.
5. Decision: Candidate presented and congregation decides whether or not to extend a call.
6. Negotiation: Details of contract finalized
7. Installation: New pastor installed
8. Start-up: Official beginning of new pastorate

- Use conflict constructively as a welcome sign of energy and vitality around those issues within the congregation.

- Teach the congregation to identify what healthy conflict is, how to live with healthy conflict and how to set clear boundaries.

- Explore the emerging identity of the congregation (as some systems put together their congregational profile) and reconsider their vision for the future.

Best Practices: Coaching Skills and Strategies

- Vision Development and Strategic Planning Coaching
- Coaching Teams and Staff
- Boundary Coaching
- Conflict Management Coaching

Additional Resources

The Interim Process: The Role of the Church and the Interim Pastor, by Carl Hart

Critical Moment of Ministry: A Change of pastors...and How it Affects Change in the Congregation, by Loren B. Mead

Temporary Shepherds: A Congregational Handbook for Interim Ministry, by Roger S. Nicholson

Beginning Ministry Together: The Alban Handbook for Clergy Transitions, by Roy Oswald, James M. Heath and Ann Heath

Pastoral Transitions: From Endings to New Beginnings, by William Bud Phillips

Leading Change in the Congregation, by Gil Rendel

Interim Ministry Network, www.imnedu.org

6. Coaching the Executive Pastor

Description of This Type of Situation

A common struggle that faces Executive Pastors is the paradigm of being a leader and a follower at the same time. This can create unnecessary friction between the Executive Pastor and the Lead Pastor. This same conflict can exist between the Executive Pastor and the pastoral staff. In addition to these relational struggles, there is the challenge of helping the Lead Pastor understand the scope of what needs to happen to bring things into fruition. Often the Executive Pastor can feel unappreciated and disrespected because of these disconnects.

Typical Coaching Scenarios

- Pastor Charles is an Executive Pastor of a fast growing church of over 1,500 attendees on a Sunday morning. In the past three years, First Church has grown by an average of 20% per year. This exponential growth has created a real demand on Pastor Charles' time. He is working an average of 65 hours a week, which includes coming home to work for an additional three to four hours per night to complete all of the accounting needs. This has been going on for two years and Pastor Charles has reached the end of his tolerance level. He has shared with his Lead Pastor that he cannot do it any longer. His Lead Pastor asks him to record his tasks for the next month, then report back to the Lead Pastor for them to discuss future options. Pastor Charles wants his Lead Pastor to trust him and support his need to hire an accountant, but feels he has fallen on deaf ears and wonders if and when this will be resolved. He knows his Lead Pastor has to process his thoughts before coming to any decisions. Pastor Charles has experienced this process to often last for weeks and even months before a decision is made.

- Over the past year, Community Church has made the move into multi-site ministry. In the transition, Pastor John, Lead Pastor, has given full authority to each multi-site Pastor to make decisions based upon the needs of each individual campus. However, in the midst of this, he has also asked Pastor Victor to oversee the financial management of each campus, as well as the coordination of all resources to ensure all campuses are consistent in their excellence and presentation on Sundays. The place where they are stuck is that Pastor Victor was not involved on the front end of the discussions, so feels that he does not have the needed information to manage the process, creating challenges in working with the Campus Pastors. Each pastor has his own vision of what projects excellence, leading to inconsistency and below standard Sunday morning experiences. Additionally, Pastor Victor is not respected as having any authority since every campus pastor has been told that they can make their own decisions about their needs.

- Pastor Shaun is the Executive Pastor of a relationally driven church that has grown to a place where the Lead Pastor cannot make personal contact with every person who attends the church. This has been the DNA of the church since its inception.

In an effort to maintain that DNA, Pastor Dan, Lead Pastor, has developed an unhealthy work ethic where he works all day and meets with people each evening and on weekends. This has had a negative effect on the energy level of Pastor Dan, and Pastor Shaun has shared his concern about the long term impact on Pastor Dan and the church. He has asked Pastor Dan to engage a personal coach, but Pastor Dan responds by saying he doesn't have time. It would only be something else that he would need to schedule and take care of. Pastor Shaun wants to help his Lead Pastor, but doesn't know what else to do.

- Pastor John is the Executive Pastor of a church where committees govern most of the decisions that guide the church. Over the years, Pastor John has grown weary of the process. He feels that he enters these meetings with some very viable options for next steps, yet comes out of them with his head low and no progress made. He feels that his Lead Pastor only serves as a pleaser to all parties. Pastor John feels alone and stuck in the middle. Pastor John just wants to serve his Lead Pastor and church to the best of his abilities, but is stuck on how he can help move the process forward.

Common Outcomes and Shifts Indicated or Desires

The goal in each of these scenarios is to help the Executive Pastor define his needs and the role he is to play in the overall picture. Coach around discovering and creating what will not only meet the needs of the Executive Pastor, but also serve the role that he plays. Help the Executive Pastor switch from one where he feels his role is to carry the vision, to one where he is supporting the vision carrier, developing a partnership between himself and the Lead Pastor. Also, touch on moving the focus from the situations that arise to the personhood of the Executive Pastor and how he adds value to their relationship and the ministry.

Best Practices: Coaching Skills and Strategies

These types of situations require focused listening skills that include deep listening of what is not said, as well as what is said. Give space for expansion on thoughts and conversation that arises. Often the underlying structure is the one that feeds into the surface. Some of these shifts can be discovered by questioning along the lines of self-awareness and Lead Pastor expectations. Help the Executive Pastor identify any limiting beliefs that may be constraining his freedom of expression with his Lead Pastor, so that authentic open communication can be developed, leading to partnership in the vision and expectations.

7. Coaching Situations in Music Ministry

A Brief Description of This Situation

Generally speaking, there are two types of Music Ministers. We will identify them as the **vocational** and the **professional volunteer**.

The **vocational types** are characterized by their high level of music education. They will have a minimum of a bachelor's degree in music, most likely with a focus in the classical repertoire and music history. They are creative types who think subjectively and value aesthetic beauty. Focused on high achievement, they are rarely satisfied with their performance but protective of their efforts.

The **professional volunteer** is someone who has limited technical background in music, but was drawn into the position by his love of ministry. He is a free spirit and highly committed to his faith and community. He is a people person, great motivator and works well as part of a team, but can experience challenges in his individual goals and personal development.

Typical Coaching Scenarios

Vocational

- They have great rapport with the choir yet frequently struggle with their relationship with the leadership.
- They very often struggle with their personal finances.
- They may be dissatisfied with their present position and are considering change.

Professional Volunteer

- They commonly struggle with their personal life and connections.
- They typically struggle with career development and future goals.
- They usually have invested in their community but may have forgotten their own personal needs.

Common Outcomes and Shifts Indicated or Desired

Vocational

FROM	TO
Isolation (single vision)	Part of a team (group vision)
Music/Aesthetic focus	Ministry/Community focus
Feeling unheard	Listening

Professional Volunteer

FROM	TO
• Them	• We (I included)
• Scattered	• Focus
• In the moment	• Long term goals

Best Practices: Coaching Skills and Strategies

Vocational

As a coach, listen: The vocational music minister feels isolated and unheard. As a coach, make an extra effort to build trust and intimacy, and make sure he feels you understand.

Coaches acknowledge jobs well done: It took a great effort to be a highly skilled professional and get to where he is. But the financial rewards are minimal. The vocational music minister desires that his work and achievements be recognized.

Coach to help him be real: His individualist self may sometimes make him lose touch with the real issues. When coaching, appropriately use direct communication to bring him back to the real world.

Professional Volunteer

As a coach, be a team player: For the Professional Volunteer Music Minister, everything is about the community and the team. You will get everything from him if he knows you are part of the team.

Coach to help and maintain focus: There is no lack of ideas here but sometimes difficulty on completion and realistic vision of future steps. Help the coachee think ahead and focus his creative mind on building a sound strategy and sequential steps.

Coach to support "who" he is: Bring it back to the "who." The Professional Volunteer Music Minister is thirsting for personal acknowledgement and esteem. Help him see the importance of putting his own oxygen mask on first before he helps others.

Additional Resources

The Church Musician—Revised Edition, by Paul Westermeyer.

Pastoral Music in Practice 5—The Pastoral Musician, Virgil C. Funk, ed.

The Ministry of Musicians, Edward J. McKenna.

8. Coaching for Career Transition

A Brief Description of This Situation

An individual seeking coaching for career transition may fall in any one of these broad categories:

1. Desire complete change of career

2. Enjoy the career they have but want to do more with it

3. Forced transition (layoff, fired)

4. Re-entering the workforce

5. Entrepreneur

Typical Coaching Scenarios

- A missionary has been serving internationally for 30 years. He/she feels the Lord's leading back to their sending country. As the missionary looks to the future, they wonder what job they can pursue and who will hire them.

- A denominational or association ministry leader seeks coaching because they feel stuck in a position that they do not enjoy. They get paid well, and that is what has kept them in their career until this point. Recently, however, the ministry leader started asking questions about why they spend time doing something that does not fulfill their passion.

- A pastor desires to move to a larger church, but keeps getting denied. The pastor enjoys the role he has but does not understand what is preventing him from receiving the larger church he seeks.

Common Outcomes and Shifts Indicated or Desired

- Maintain current career but at a new company/in a new environment.
- Identify the intersection of a client's knowledge, skills, passions and desired work environment to discover a new career path.
- Identify unique personal characteristics and transferable skills required to achieve the desired career outcome.

- Identify a new career path and the steps required to attain the desired result.
- Identify gaps in competencies and strategize steps to bridge the gaps.
- Identify interpersonal characteristics that affect the client's potential.
- Recognize the decisions that led to the current situation and evaluate them for potential growth.

Best Practices: Coaching Skills and Strategies

- Consider all aspects of the individual, not just their skills. Look at an individual's values, personality, passions and aspirations.

- Identify external filters that cloud the client's judgment. Encourage coaching sessions to be explorations of all possibilities.

- Encourage research into various career options. Ensure that the client understands what is important to them in their future career and research with those goals in mind.

- Utilize assessments as a starting point but do not let them dictate the end result of the client's career path.

Additional Resources

National Society of Career Management—www.nsocm.com

MindTools—www.mindtools.com

CPP—www.cpp.com

TTI Performance Systems, Ltd.—www.ttidisc.com

The Riley Guide—www.rileyguide.com

Bureau of Labor Statistics—www.bls.gov

O*Net Online—online.onetcenter.org

Now, Discover Your Strengths, by Marcus Buckingham and Donald O. Clifton, Ph.D.

StrengthsFinder 2.0, by Tom Rath

What Color Is Your Parachute?, by Richard Nelson Bolles

9. Coaching in Pre-marital and Marriage Sessions

A Brief Description of This Situation

Premarital. Often couples come together with a desire to marry without ever considering their backgrounds or differences. This can bring immovable barriers that can become issues that not only can sabotage the marriage, but can poison the relationship if not attended to in the beginning. Often the couples get to an impasse that they cannot move past without coaching assistance. In order to help them move forward, they need a coach to help them see the dream marriage that God has planned for them.

Marriage. Too often good marriages fall into ruts that couples thought they would never experience. They think, "Not us, we will be different"; yet life's paths carried them to bland places that began with good intent. Many of these are good paths, such as raising children and serving the church, which lead to good things, yet there is something missing. Couples want that dream they had when they said, "I Do," that leads to married life full of vibrancy and passion.

Typical Coaching Scenarios

John and Mary have made the decision to spend the rest of their lives together in marriage. They share with their pre-marital coaches that they can't live without each other. However, in their most recent discussions, they have found that their views of extended family relationships differ significantly. John left home when he was 18 to join the military and Mary has always been a home body who loves spending time with family. He has been looking forward to building a dream marriage where he and Mary will establish their own family, full of new traditions and values. Mary, on the other hand, has been looking forward to a marriage where she and John will encompass their parents in all aspects of their lives and incorporate John into the family traditions she experienced as a child. She thinks this will help John get closer to his parents as well. John is resistant and has no desire to do so. He feels he has broken free from the parental controls he experienced as a youth and never wants to go back. They are distraught and have no idea how to move past this obstacle.

Justin and Jessica want to get married yet realize they come from two totally different backgrounds. Justin has been married before and comes from a history of divorce, where his dad has been married three times and his mom is on her second marriage. But, it doesn't stop there, his siblings as well as aunts and uncles have a history of divorce. However, Jessica doesn't have any divorce in her family history. Justin wants this marriage to last forever and not repeat the mistakes from his first marriage. He has no example of how to build a marriage to last. They want to take appropriate steps, but have no idea where to begin.

Joe and Cathy have been married for seven years and have hit an obstacle. Joe has been busy building his career, working late and taking customers out in the evenings. Mary feels that Joe has left her to raise their three kids on her own. She's not at the end of her rope, but certainly feels things have to change. She dreamed of spending her life with Joe, not just her kids. She wants her husband to make her number one, as it was when they we dating. Both she and Joe want what they had in the beginning, but neither of them knows how to get it back.

Mark and Annie have been happily married for 22 years and now are empty nesters. Over the 22 years, their marriage has been good, but now that it is just the two of them, good is not good enough. They have always dreamed of having that great marriage that others envy and are ready to do whatever it takes to get there. They have contemplated counseling, but that doesn't seem to fit since they don't have marital issues, they just want more.

Common Outcomes and Shifts Indicated or Desired

A common outcome for each of these scenarios is to have both individuals work toward the same direction and goal. Shifts needed would include identifying the limiting beliefs that are keeping the couple from moving from their current situation. Help them discover how they can shift from the past and into walking in the hope and vision that they have for their marriage.

Best Practices: Coaching Skills and Strategies

In couples coaching, whether pre-marital or marriage, it is essential to help each couple identify what they want their marriage to look like before they can have the confidence to pull themselves out of the quicksand. Their current situation always seems more powerful than the dream ahead of them. Help them paint the picture of what they want and then to paint the path to take them to their dream. Utilize questioning to create an awareness of the path needed. Help them identify their limiting beliefs about their marriage potential to navigate to new beliefs about themselves and marriage.

Summary

In this chapter we have looked at several coaching scenarios that are common in ministry coaching. There are a multitude of others that you will encounter as you coach. It is important to remember these are generalizations. These are given as examples of what you may encounter as you coach and to open the door to seeing more possibilities. Being curious, exploring strengths, defining vision, exploring options and aligning with our individual coachees are all important parts of powerful coaching. Each situation is as different as are the people that come for coaching. Coaching is not about consulting or prescribing a plan. Coaching is about bringing out the best in our clients and frequently those around them, using their personal strengths and gifts, and helping them move forward in their unique circumstances to their vision.

Chapter Four

Coaching Intact Teams and Groups

Author's Note: An additional resource for this chapter is found on the Coaching4Clergy website at www.coaching4clergy.com. Download the free e-book entitled: *The E3 Church: Empowered, Effective and Entrepreneurial Leadership,* by J. Val Hastings.

What are the Benefits of Coaching Intact Teams and Groups in a Ministry Setting?

Leaders who use a coach approach generally observe the following about their intact teams and groups:

- More participation of all team members
- Better solutions
- Facilitative vs. directive approach
- Better "buy-in" to solutions and their execution
- Leadership and skill development of team members
- Shared leadership
- Shared responsibility
- Shared accountability
- Stronger functioning teams

Leaders using a coach approach with their teams and groups generally find they, as leader, do the following:

- Lead with questions vs. statements/directives.
- Look for the answers within the group vs. assume they do not have the answer.
- Promote action and accountability on an individual and team level.
- Spend more time listening and less time talking.
- View their role as "catalyst" vs. "designer."

GENERAL INFORMATION ABOUT INTACT TEAMS AND GROUPS

Different Types of Intact Church Teams and Groups

Intact ministry teams are groups that work together as a team for an extended period of time. They usually identify themselves as a team and have common goals. Examples include:

- **Staff Team.** Usually a paid team that is responsible for all church functions.
- **Accountability Groups**. Individuals who meet together on a regular basis to hold each other accountable to living out biblical principles.
- **Small Groups**. Also called Life Groups. The focus is on individual life change and transformation.
- **Community Groups.** Individuals who meet together to study the bible or to meet a need in the larger community.
- **Church Committees.** Individuals who serve together on a team that supports the church and the church staff in the work of the church.

Fixed Content Versus Flexible Content

Fixed Content

Fixed content generally refers to a team working with any of the following:

- Standard content base—such as bible study, committee documents
- Fixed goals
- Defined roles

When coaching a team or group with fixed content, you generally coach from the listening, questioning and action/accountability perspective. Strong listening skills along with powerful questions are most effective.

- Frequently, the best approach is to ask questions from the content and then use your deep listening skills to understand the reactions to the information being presented.
- Utilize your action and accountability skills with the content you are using/studying to ensure learning is implemented. Ask powerful questions of the group.

- Listen for the limiting beliefs and false assumptions of the team or group.

- Share your perspectives and observations.

Flexible Content

Flexible content generally refers to situations where the content is:

- Minimal or virtually non-existent

- Roles are not defined

- Goals are not clearly defined

When coaching teams and groups with flexible content, it is important to establish the coaching agreement with the group. This includes the area of focus, plus the agreed upon results and take-away for the group.

The Stages of Teams and Groups

Knowing the stage of development of a team or group can be useful to the coach. Knowing team development can provide clues that explain team behavior. Dr. Bruce Tuckman developed the Five Stages of Team Dynamics. These include:

- Forming

- Storming

- Norming

- Performing

- Adjourning (in the 1970s)

Another approach to understanding team development is to view the team from the human development perspective. This approach would then include the following stages of development:

- Childhood

- Adolescence

- Young Adulthood

- Middle Adulthood

- Seasoned/Sr. Adulthood

The stage of team or group development will inform your coaching approach. For example:

Forming/Childhood. At this stage the team is relatively new. Individuals are just beginning to get to know each other as they work toward their identity as a group. Generally, the group avoids controversy and decisions as they attempt to develop relationships and identity.

As the Coach:

- Your job is to put them at ease and create a safe space. Encourage the team to make decisions and be open to having in-depth discussions. Employ your questioning and active listening skills.

- Work with the group to clarify goals. In this stage there is a high dependence on the leader for guidance and direction. The team has little understanding or perspective on team goals, other than those received from the leader. Individual roles and responsibilities are unclear, as is the team's purpose and objective.

Storming/Adolescence. This is the stage of development where team members become disillusioned and often "check out" of the group because competition and conflict are occurring.

As the Coach:

- One of your roles is to help the team traverse the rocky path to being a fully functioning team. The team will often have difficulty coming to decisions and members will have a tendency to "jockey" for position as they work to establish their roles on the team.

- It is at this stage in the process where the leader will be challenged by team members and resistance is frequently highest.

- Acknowledge and look for the greatness in the leader and team members.

Norming/Young Adulthood. At this stage in the process, the team's ability to collaborate effectively increases. Trust begins to actively develop among team members. The team is receptive to new ideas as well as the ideas of others both inside and outside the team. The team discusses and develops its processes and working style. Agreement and consensus begins to emerge within the team, roles and responsibilities become clearer and accepted, and "big" decisions are often made by group consensus. Smaller decisions may be delegated to individuals and/or small teams within the group.

As the Coach:

- Encourage the team to work together, explore alternatives and work on solutions within the established team ground rules.

- Partner with the team to help them reach their fullest potential. Keep the team on task.

- Encourage the team to engage in fun and social activities.

Performing/Middle Adulthood. In this stage, the team has learned how to tap into the strengths of each team member. The team members show loyalty, trust and openness. The team exhibits a high level of creativity and productivity. Differences in opinion are viewed as a spring board for innovation.

The team is strategically focused in its shared vision and is clear about what needs to be accomplished. The team has a high degree of autonomy. Disagreements occur but now they are resolved within the team in a positive manner. Team members look after each other and the team needs very little direction from the leader.

As the Coach:

- Acknowledge and praise team members on their accomplishment and encourage them to do the same with each other.

- Capitalize on the loyalty and productivity of the team to maximize performance.

- Take time out to evaluate team effectiveness and encourage team members to do the same individually and within the team.
- Find ways to motivate the team to peak performance.

Adjourning/Seasoned Adulthood. This stage usually occurs when a team has a finite life (i.e. Pastor Search Team). When this stage occurs, the team recognizes that the project is near completion and that their team will disband soon. It can be bittersweet for team members.

As the Coach:

- Help the team process what they have learned and accomplished.
- Capitalize on what has been achieved and how they have served others.
- Encourage the team to celebrate.
- Realize this may be difficult for some team members as close bonds have been forged.
- Recognize some team members may find this transition difficult.

Coaching Strategies for Intact Teams and Groups

Distinctions and Shifts

The following are several key distinctions to be aware of when coaching teams and groups:

- Working Harder vs. Producing Results
- A Team of Individuals vs. a Team that is Connected
- Definition by Challenge vs. Definition by Vision
- Efficient vs. Effective
- Ministry by Default vs. Ministry by Design
- Adversarial Thinking vs. Strategic Thinking

The following are key distinctions to use when coaching the team or group leader: *Source: The E3 Church: Empowered, Effective and Entrepreneurial Leadership*

Shift 1: From Diagnosing to Developing

- Learn to help others develop vs. diagnosing and solving their problems.
- Coach them to diagnosis their problems and then partner with them to develop and support their progress forward.

Shift 2: From Doing to Empowering

- Leaders must stop doing so others can start doing.
- Empower and develop others to "do."

Shift 3: From Telling to Exploring

- Move from "telling" to "asking."
- Explore possibilities.

Shift 4: From Mindlessness to Mindfulness

- *Transactional* interactions to *Transformational* interactions.
- Being aware and intentional.

Shift 5: From Excellence to Effectiveness

- Ready, FIRE, Aim to Ready, AIM, Fire.
- Doing something well vs. making a difference.

Shift 6: From Professional to Entrepreneur

- Status Quo to Change Catalyst.

- Risk Adverse to Embracing Risk.
- Taking It Forward.

Coach the WHO of the Group or Team

- Listen for the WHO of the group.

- Notice values and beliefs.

- Hear the group story (without getting hooked into their story).

- Avoid the tendency to coach the individual team members.

- Ask:
  - What are 10 things I need to know about this team in order to coach you?
  - What stage of development is this group in? (See above information on the stages of team development.)
  - What should I never, ever, ever ask or request of this group?
  - If this group suddenly disbanded, who would notice? What wouldn't get done?

Work the Gap

Here and Now versus Then and There

- Request that the group or team develop a current and realistic picture.
- Request that the group also create a future, ideal picture.
- Ask the group to identify the gap that exists between the current and future picture.
- Begin developing a plan of action to bridge the gap.
- Identify sabotage. When, where and how does sabotage usually show up.

- Create a system of accountability and follow-up to ensure that the plan of action is implemented.

Three Questions Model

- What's happening in this group? (Current reality picture.)
- What's possible in this group? (Put on your rose-colored glasses.)
- What steps can we take to move forward as a group? (Today. Right now.)

Eliminate—Delegate—Systematize

Most individuals can eliminate, delegate or systematize about 50% of what they are currently doing. The same is often true of groups.

Imagine how much more effective and productive your team could be if it were responsible for 50% less. If your team eliminated, delegated and systematized it could:

- Really focus on what is most important.
- Shorten the time and frequency of team meetings.
- Make real, tangible progress forward.
- Develop a team mentality.
- Share the work load.
- Be proactive versus reactive.
- Have fun!

Chapter Five

Creating New Awareness — Coaching on Limiting Beliefs and False Assumptions

Definitions

Belief—A certainty or truth accepted by an individual or a group.

Assumption—Believed to be true without proof, or the proof is situational or circumstantial.

General Comments

- Beliefs and assumptions are not necessarily good or bad.
- Beliefs and assumptions are 100% true for those who believe them.
- There are usually stories that support our beliefs and assumptions.
- Everyone has beliefs and assumptions AND they show up in coaching all the time.
- Beliefs and assumptions are powerful. They can:
    - Propel us forward OR paralyze us.
    - Expand our options OR limit our choices.
    - Rally one to take initiative OR cause one to throw in the towel.

Examples of Beliefs and Assumptions

- The world is flat!
- Nothing ever really changes.
- They will think that I'm stupid.
- I don't know as much as they do.
- I'm stupid.
- We really don't have a choice.
- Change is always difficult.
- Change takes time.
- I cannot lead.
- We're not as big as the other church in town.
- We don't have the right pastor.
- The church is out-dated.

How Do We Explode Beliefs That Limit and Assumptions That Are False?

Listen for limiting beliefs and false assumptions

- Listen deeply. Look for them.
- Assume that everyone has limiting beliefs and false assumptions.
- Scratch below the surface of what the person is saying. "Get" the person.
- Identify the story or inner tape that has been created.

Be curious and inquisitive

- Limiting beliefs and false assumptions have gained power because they have gone unquestioned.
- Ask open-ended, powerful questions.
- Invite them to engage their mind.
- Request that they play and have fun. Play engages curiosity. A person that is having fun is more likely to experiment.

Curiosity as we age. Eight hundred and seventy children were tracked regarding curiosity at age 6 and then again at age 16.

- At 8 years of age, 84% of the children were in curiosity mode.
- At 16 years of age, 7% of the children were in curiosity mode.
- Over a span of 8 years, most children stopped being curious.

Express appreciation

- A 5 to 1 ratio of appreciation to criticism helps people think. (*Time to Think*, by Nancy Kline.)
- Change takes place best in a context of genuine praise.
- Look for the greatness in others and stop trying to fix people.

Ask the incisive question

In her book *Time to Think*, Nancy Kline offers a simple yet profound method of dealing with limiting beliefs and false assumptions. Her method involves asking the Incisive Question.

Her methods include the following:

1. **What do you want to achieve?**
   Begin by helping the person get clarity around what it is that they really, REALLY want to accomplish.

2. **What might you be assuming that is stopping you from achieving your goal?**
   Other questions to ask include: What are you assuming about this goal? What is your belief about this goal? There are reasons why the individual or group hasn't achieved their goal(s). Help them identify obstacles, especially beliefs and assumptions.

   I was facilitating a visioning retreat for a faith community when all of a sudden the momentum and involvement stopped. When I inquired, several leaders said that this was the third time in three years that they had undergone a visioning process. A key leader stated: "The previous two attempts failed and we all believe that the same will happen again."

3. **Articulate the POSITIVE OPPOSITE of your limiting belief or false assumption.**
   This is often a difficult task for an individual or team to do, but press them to articulate the positive opposite. Once articulated, ask them to write it down and say it several times. You are now ready to craft the Incisive Question.

4. **The Incisive Question contains the following**:
   If you knew… *Insert the Positive Opposite* …, what action would you take? What would be different?

5. **Write down the action you will take.**

Chapter Six

Establishing Yourself as a Coach

If you have gotten this far in your journey, you have experienced the power of coaching both in your own life and you have sought to coach others. Now you are standing on the edge asking God, "What next?"

I have found that many in ministry believe that successfully transitioning into something other than local church ministry, let alone launching a new business, was next to impossible. Plus, if you are lucky enough to escape, the odds are it won't last.

As I experienced the power of coaching and began to see its transformational impact on others, it caused me to reflect further about my own transition into full-time coaching and how I could help others do the same. As a coach, mentor-coach and coach-trainer, I have had the opportunity to help others hone their coaching skills, as well as launch a successful coaching business. Most of these individuals have been spiritual leaders **hoping to escape**.

This resource is specifically written to help you successfully develop and launch a sustainable coaching business. The materials included in this chapter are a compilation of my years of coaching, mentor-coaching and coach-training. While it is not an exhaustive resource, it is a collection of best practices, strategies and shifts to help you successfully develop your own coaching business.

Topics covered in this chapter include:

- Val's Top Ten Checklist
- Typical Transition Strategies
- What's the Z?
- The Upside-Down Funnel Approach
- Key Shifts for the Coach
- Your Relationship with Money
- How to Speed Things Up?
- Mistakes and Myths

VAL'S TOP TEN CHECKLIST

Let's begin with a checklist. The following checklist is designed to give you a quick snapshot of how you are doing, as well as identify what needs work. Using the checklist below, check-off those items that apply to your current coaching business. Let's get an accurate picture of your current reality.

1. I am able to say "I am a coach!" with a straight face.

2. I have identified four to seven connectors who have agreed to help me build my coaching business. (Connectors are people that know how to make things happen.)

3. I am working with a mentor-coach who has their own successful, sustainable coaching business.

4. I am comfortable talking to others about money.

5. I have a financial reserve and a financial plan.

6. I know that coaching is legitimate, even if people don't get it.

7. I have set up a coaching environment that helps me be fully present with those I coach.

8. I have a good headset, computer and internet service. I also have a back-up telephone or mobile phone.

9. I am ready to coach. That is, I have a professional-looking welcome letter, website, business cards, coaching agreement and payment process. I have automated as much of this as I can.

10. I regularly follow up with prospective and previous coachees.

11. BONUS: *I regularly celebrate my successes, no matter how small or large.*

TYPICAL TRANSITION STRATEGIES

How Do You Enter a Swimming Pool?

Consider the different ways that people enter a swimming pool. Some people jump right in, while others ease their way into the water. Still others never leave the kiddie pool. How do you enter a swimming pool?

Just as there are different ways to enter a pool, there are also different ways to transition to full-time coaching. Consider the following approaches. Which one is best for you? What are the implications of your approach? What are the benefits of each approach?

Jump into the Deep End of the Pool. Jump right in!

- Quit your job and start a coaching practice, or
- Get a no brainer job so you can focus on coaching.

Slide into the Pool. First your big toe, then slowly enter the pool.

- Work full-time and coach part-time.
- Eventually work part-time and coach part-time.
- Gradually add more and more clients.

Bring the Pool to You. Incorporate coaching into your current position.

- Talk to your employer, supervisor or board about incorporating coaching into what you already do.
- Develop an internal coaching position.
- Bloom right where you are planted.

Swim in Someone Else's Pool. Partner, collaborate or join another coach's team.

- Work for another coach.
- Pool your resources with other coaches.

WHAT'S THE Z?

Begin with the End in Mind

It's not uncommon for a coach to forget about developing a complete vision of their coaching business. We coach others to begin with a clear picture of the end. Without a bull's eye on the target, how will you know if you have been successful?

"What's the Z" is about beginning with the end in mind. Identifying the "Z" includes articulating the purpose of your coaching business, as well as painting the picture and defining what your business looks like. Consider the following questions:

- How do you define full-time coaching?
- What would an ideal week (or month) look like for you as a full-time coach?
- Describe the ideal individual or team that you are coaching.
- What are your beliefs and assumptions about full-time coaching?
- Of the beliefs you have identified, which are limiting you? Which are serving you well? What new beliefs do you want to add?

- Where are you in the process of transitioning to full-time coaching? What are the next two or three key steps?

THE UPSIDE-DOWN FUNNEL APPROACH

Most people, when launching a business, adopt the Funnel Approach. This approach, like a funnel, is wide at the top and narrow at the bottom. Using this approach, an individual attempts to contact, connect, network and market to as many people and organizations as possible. This approach attempts to touch a large number of people (wide end of the funnel) and usually yields a few people (narrow end of the funnel).

The Upside-Down Funnel Approach literally inverts the traditional approach. Instead of a mass approach, which is very impersonal, this approach advocates connecting with a much smaller group and investing in them. I contend that all that is needed in this approach are four to seven really good "Connectors". Investing heavily in a few people (narrow end of the funnel) yields much (wide end of the funnel).

Who are connectors? Where do you find them? Connectors are individuals who know how to make things happen. Every organization has them. These are the Paul Reveres versus the William Dawes from our history books. Both of these individuals were asked to spread the word about impending danger. People listened to Paul and paid little attention to William.

One of my original connectors brought me 34 coachees all at once. While subsequent connectors haven't delivered this high number at once, they regularly help me secure larger contracts and introduce me to other connectors.

Here's the strategy I recommend:

- **Identify Your Connectors.** Sit down and begin listing names. They are there. Comb through your address book and contact list.

- **Invest in Your Connectors.** Connect with your connectors. Develop the relationship further. **Add Value to their world.** This is what they are looking for. I've coached many of my connectors, done favors for them and befriended them. **Adding value is their currency.**

- **Be on the look-out for new Connectors.** I am always looking for my next connector. Early on I thought that connectors had to be people that I knew well. That's a myth. Connectors, by their very nature, like expanding their connections. It's what makes them so effective. **I have several connectors that I have never met in person, who don't really know me, but know another connector who recommended me.**

KEY SHIFTS

As You Transition to Full-Time Coaching

As coaches, we know about shifts. We coach individuals and teams on key shifts all the time. Shifts are internal (or, below the surface) changes and reorientations that dramatically alter one's approach or perspective, resulting in a significantly different outcome. As coaches, we also have shifts. Consider the following key shifts as you develop your coaching business.

Shift: Hobby Versus Business

Coaching as a hobby is fun, intriguing and interesting. As a hobby, you immerse yourself in coaching when you want to. Making money is optional; in fact, the investment in most hobbies is far greater than the return. And that's okay. It's a hobby.

Coaching as a business is also fun, intriguing and interesting…and more. As a business owner, you are monitoring investment and return. Making money is NOT optional. There are intentional processes and approaches in place to further develop and sustain the business for the benefit of the coach and coachee.

This shift impacts your decision-making process. Decisions now include:

- ROI (Return On Investment).
- Will this bring me closer to my vision?
- Financial obligations and responsibilities.
- Course corrections and partnerships

How would you rate yourself regarding this shift?

Hobby <——————————————————————————————> Business

Shift: Free-Based Coaching vs. Fee-Based Coaching

One of the places that many newer coaches have difficulty, especially those with a ministry background, is charging a fee. For many this is a difficult shift. New coaches want to know the secret of charging a fee, especially when they hear the fee structures of seasoned coaches. Questions abound:

- What's a good coaching fee for a newer coach?
- How do you ask for a fee?

- How do you explain what coaching is?
- And, what about the rejection? How do you handle the dreaded "No"?

Consider the following comments regarding this shift:

- As I increased in my coaching confidence and competency, my fees increased.
- Charging a fee for coaching is more for the benefit of the coachee, than the benefit of the coach. Coachees who are financially invested in coaching tend to approach the coaching process very differently than pro-bono coachees. In fact, my frustration with pro-bono coachees helped me make this shift. Those who pay for coaching:
  - Show up prepared and ready to fully engage in the coaching process. They are also much more likely to have taken the agreed upon action steps.
  - Paying coachees are willing to go deeper in the coaching conversation.
  - They value coaching and their coach.
- There are really only four reasons people say NO:
  - NO Need
  - NO Money
  - NO Hurry
  - NO Credibility
    By Ken Abrams (www.kenabrams.com)

BONUS: The fifth reason people say NO.

Sometimes when a person says NO, what they are really saying is NOT YET. When we hear them say NO, we stop all contact and follow through. We draw a line through their name and move on to the next person. And that's where it ends. And yet, what is really needed by the prospective coachee is time and space to think and prepare before they are ready to begin the coaching process. They are looking for periodic follow through, additional value and connection.

Skillful listening, practice and trial-and-error enable the coach to hear the distinction between NO and NOT YET. Identifying the value-to-add is part of this process. Discerning the frequency and type of follow-up are critical, as well as listening past the NO. **Follow-Through Matters.**

Shift: Selling vs. Adding Value

I don't sell. Let me say it again, I don't sell!

A common myth among many newer coaches is that you have to be able to sell in order to have a full-time coaching business. Or, that you have to be an expert at marketing. Nothing could be further from the truth. In fact, my experience has been that traditional sales and marketing approaches do not work, and frequently distract newer coaches from investing in steps that will further develop their coaching business.

Rather than selling, this shift is about identifying what's really, REALLY needed. This shift is about eliminating questions like:

- How do I convince people to purchase what I'm selling?
- How do I get them to want what I'm offering?

One of my favorite quotes expresses this so effectively:

> *Your opinion, although interesting, is irrelevant!*
> (The Tuned-In Mantra)

Tuned In authors Craig Stull, Phil Myers and David Meerman Scott refer to this as understanding the **Buyer Personas**, i.e., truly understanding who will buy and invest in what you are offering.

> By truly understanding the market problems that your products and services solve for your buyer personas, you transform your marketing from mere product-specific, egocentric gobbledygook that only you understand and care about into valuable information people are eager to consume and that they use to make the choice to do business with your organization.
> —David Meerman Scott, *World Wide Wave*, p. 24

The **TUNED IN PROCESS** is simple to learn and provides a model for marketing strategy (Craig Stull, Phil Myers and David Meerman Scott).

Step 1: **Find Unresolved Problems** (to know what market and which product or service to focus on)

Step 2: **Understand Buyer Personas** (to understand who will buy what you are offering)

Step 3: **Quantify the Impact** (to know if you have a potential winner)

Step 4: **Create Breakthrough Experiences** (to build a competitive advantage)

Step 5: **Articulate Powerful Ideas** (to establish the memorable concepts that match up with the problems people have)

Step 6: **Establish Authentic Connections** (to tell your buyers that you've solved their problems so they buy from you)

Shift: I Am Almost a Coach vs. I Am a Coach

Someone that I recently mentor-coached offered the following statement about my success:

The reason that Val is successful as a coach is because
Val is sold on the value of his coaching.

See yourself as a coach! The ability to say and believe that you are a coach is more important than you think. This is one of those times when a little overconfidence can actually help.

YOUR RELATIONSHIP WITH MONEY

Strange as it may seem, your relationship with money will impact the success and sustainability of your coaching business. In my mentor-coaching, it is common for newer coaches to totally gloss over their current and future financial picture. Another common scenario among newer coaches is to be completely overwhelmed or intimidated by the financial components of a full-time coaching business.

I encourage newer coaches to explore their relationship with money. In many cases, newer coaches end up involved in a money make-over regarding their relationship with money. Here are a couple of ways to initiate a Money Make-Over.

- What were your family of origin's beliefs and practices regarding money?
  - How well are these currently serving you?
- What is your current belief about money?
  - How well will your current belief about money serve you as you develop a full-time coaching business?
  - What new beliefs and practices regarding money do you need to develop?
- Define a healthy relationship with money. Who do you know who has a healthy relationship with money?

- Take stock of your current financial picture. (An honest snapshot)
  - What are your current expenses and income?
  - What are your anticipated expenses?
  - Remember to include: taxes, health insurance, liability insurance, disability insurance, memberships, etc. Don't forget LLC, incorporation or non-profit status.
  - How many clients do you need to coach to meet, and exceed, your expenses?
  - When will your clients pay you? How will they pay you? How much of this can you automate?
  - How much financial reserve do you currently have? How much is needed?
- Develop a financial budget and plan. Stick to it. Regularly review it.

HOW TO SPEED THINGS UP?

Below is a list of proven best practices for accelerating your transition to full-time coaching:

- Coach, Coach and Coach.
- Connect, Connect and Connect.
- Identify your Buyer Persona (understand who will buy what you are offering).
- Develop a strong personal foundation.
- Rub shoulders with other new coaches who are doing the same thing.
- Identify administrative supports and structures. Remember, you don't have to do it all.
- Decide how and when your coachees will pay for your services.
- Automate as much as possible.
- Before anyone hires you as their coach, create your welcome kit, coaching agreement and prospect letter.
- Have in place a website and business card.
- Will you be creating a newsletter? Hard-copy or email newsletter? Frequency of distribution?
- Hire a mentor coach.
- Develop relationships with seasoned, successful coaches for mutual support.
- Ahead of time, develop your elevator speech.

I help people get the results they want. I am a coach.

MISTAKES AND MYTHS

When developing a full-time coaching business:

- Family and friends may not regard coaching as a viable business. This can easily discourage a new coach. **Ask for the support and encouragement of your family and friends**.

- You will feel overwhelmed, discouraged and stressed by how much you don't know or because the transition is moving along slower than you anticipated. **Work with a Mentor-Coach! Rub shoulders with other coaches**.

- Stop stressing yourself financially. This is a major de-motivator. Even though you may not want to entertain the idea of **keeping your day job**—just do it!

- Don't fill your coaching business for the sake of filling your business. Identify the people and organizations that you really, REALLY want to coach. Seek them out. **Be selective in who you coach**.

- It takes more time to build a practice than you think it should. **Be patient and give yourself time**.

- Realize that you're starting a new business, not just getting a new job, starting a hobby or just improving yourself. **You are an entrepreneur!** Actually, a solo-preneur.

- Those who know me best will be more likely to hire me or promote my business. Actually, my experience has been the exact opposite. **Over 95% of those I coach I have never met before, and never have a face-to-face meeting**. Plus, those who have been most helpful in building my coaching business have been new connectors that I have never met in person.

- Identify and address your limiting beliefs and false assumptions about developing a full-time coaching business. Common limiting beliefs include:
  - No one will hire me because…
  - People won't really pay for coaching.
  - I can't sell.
  - I'm just a…pastor, etc.

Chapter Seven

Developing a Solid Personal Foundation

OBJECTIVE

The objective of this chapter is twofold:

- To assist the newer coach in the development of their own solid personal foundation.
- To provide the newer coach with practical discussion, techniques and insights for developing a solid personal foundation in their coachees.

This chapter will cover several areas:

- What is a Solid Personal Foundation?
- How Satisfied Are You?
- Sabbath, Rest and Solitude
- Caring for Yourself
- No More Tolerations
- Experiencing God

WHAT IS A SOLID PERSONAL FOUNDATION?

A Solid Personal Foundation is an intentional decision to live your life in a way that will support you to be your very best (i.e. be at the top of your game). It is an intentional investment in yourself so you can experience the abundant life Jesus spoke of in John 10:10b. Using the analogy of a house, your personal foundation is the actual foundation upon which your "house" is built. The foundation is comprised of three main components:

- Your relationship with God
- Your relationship with Yourself
- Your relationship with Others (especially family and friends)

A Strong Personal Foundation is PUTTING ON YOUR
OXYGEN MASK FIRST; you are then better able to care for
and lead those around you.

Example from Jesus

Jesus modeled for us a Solid Personal Foundation. Jesus understood that powerful doing flowed from powerful being.

Ten Things Jesus Did:

1. Jesus walked.

2. Jesus hung out with friends.

3. He read the scriptures.

4. He took naps.

5. He walked away from the crowds, even though there was more he could do.

6. Jesus got mad. (Good and angry.)

7. He went to church.

8. Jesus prayed.

9. Jesus had fun. (He went to parties. He played with children.)

10. Jesus took his time and paced himself.

Your Personal Vision/Life Purpose

A strong sense of vision and purpose is what moves us forward in our life. To move forward effectively and with energy, we need to know what we want and have a clear vision on how to move positively in that direction. Too often, we move through life letting others choose our purpose or not clearly articulating our personal vision/purpose. This path often robs us of our energy, passion and performance.

Consider the following questions:

1. What are your strengths?

2. Where is your passion?

3. What need in the world are you drawn to meet?

4. What impact do you find yourself consistently having on people?

5. What life story do you want to tell?

6. What is your personal vision/purpose statement?

Client Application

1. How would you use a vision/purpose statement with your clients?

2. How would you guide them through the process?

3. When would you use this in your coaching process?

4. What are indicators that your clients need to work on their vision?

5. What are questions you would ask your clients about their vision?

HOW SATISFIED ARE YOU?

Wheel Exercise

The "Wheel" exercise provides a visual representation of how satisfied you are with various key aspects of your life. It reflects what you value most and how you are expending your energy.

Directions: The eight sections in the Wheel represent balance. Seeing the center of the wheel as zero and the outer edges as 10, rank your level of satisfaction with each life area by drawing a straight or curved line to create a new outer edge.

Consider the following questions:

1. Why do you think the areas you marked as most satisfied are that way?

2. Where are the areas you would like to target for improvement?

3. What steps can you take right away to improve those areas?

4. If you marked any areas as a 1 or 2, have you given up hope?

Client Application

1. When would you use this exercise with your client?

2. What are the drawbacks of this exercise?

3. How would you unpack the "Wheel" exercise with your clients?

SABBATH, REST AND SOLITUDE

The Old and New Testaments are filled with references to the importance of Sabbath, Rest and Solitude. Jesus frequently modeled these throughout his life and ministry.

Let's explore these areas more completely:

- Why are Sabbath, Rest and Solitude recurring themes in the scriptures? What's so important about them?
- In what ways to do you practice Sabbath and Rest?
- What are the challenges you face in regularly practicing Sabbath and Rest?
- What would be different if Sabbath and Rest were practiced regularly?
- What are the unique benefits of Solitude?
- What distracts or derails you from time alone?
- What steps can you take in these areas? Right now? Today?

Client Application

1. What are the signs and signals that Sabbath, Rest and Solitude are key issues for those you coach?

2. How would you introduce this to your coachee?

3. What "push-back" would you expect from your coachee in these areas?

CARING FOR YOURSELF

People lead busy lives.

It is common for people to ignore their own self-care.

Frequently, people will state that they feel guilty when they take time for themselves.

Many people neglect caring for themselves.

Saying Yes and No

Self-care involves saying "yes" and "no" to various requests in life. It also involves a conscious awareness of when and what to say "yes" and "no" to. Complete the following exercise as it relates to your life and being your very best.

I will say YES to the following:

_____
_____
_____

Which means I will say NO to the following:

_____
_____
_____

I will say NO to the following:

_____
_____
_____

So I can say YES to the following:

_____
_____
_____

Healthy Practices

Identify healthy practices that will promote self-care for you. For example: Going to bed earlier, creating regular breaks or time outs throughout the day, sitting at the dinner table to eat. These simple, regular practices can actually make a difference in the quality of your life. Go ahead, identify your healthy practices:

1. _____
   _____
2. _____
   _____

3. _____
   _____

4. _____
   _____

5. _____
   _____

6. _____
   _____

7. _____
   _____

8. _____
   _____

9. _____
   _____

10._____
   _____

Client Application

1. What are the indicators your coachee needs to be more intentional about their own personal care?

2. How would you introduce self-care to your coachee?

3. How and when would you introduce the healthy practices exercise?

4. What other self-care resources and exercises would you offer your coachee?

NO MORE TOLERATIONS!

One of the quickest ways to feel better, have more energy and get results is to identify and eliminate your tolerations.

We all have tolerations!

In fact, most people aren't even aware of all that they are tolerating.

We're often aware of our bigger tolerations. For example, a job that is frustrating, the bad habits of a family member, or paying taxes.

What we are often unaware of are the rest of our tolerations. The ones that are below the surface. They nag at us and put us in a bad mood. Think of these tolerations as "white noise" or background music. They're there. They have an impact on us. And we usually don't notice it.

In this exercise, identify as many tolerations as you can. Start writing them down. Big ones. Little ones. People, places, things. Keep a list. Then, over the next week, continue adding to the list. If you're like most people, by the end of the week, you'll have a long list of tolerations.

Tolerations take a toll on a person. No wonder we don't feel at our best.

Go ahead. Get started on your list.

Here are some examples:

- A corner piece of wallpaper that has come loose.
- A car radio that doesn't work.
- Wrinkled clothing.
- A neighbor's loud car.
- Dirty dishes left in the sink.
- A crooked picture.
- Holes in several of your socks.
- A chatty co-worker who won't stop talking.
- A burned out light bulb in the attic.
- Photos from a vacation 10 years ago that haven't been put in the photo album.

Eliminate Your Tolerations:

- Identity the top 5, 10 or 20 tolerations that you could easily and immediately eliminate. And "just do it." Eliminate them.
- Look for themes and groups on your toleration list. Sometimes by eliminating one or two tolerations, you can actually get rid of a whole group.
- What needs immediate attention?
- What is the cost of all that you are tolerating?
- Who, or what, is the biggest energy drain on your list?
- What current habits or daily routines are NOT enriching your life?
- Where are your boundaries weak?
- What are ways to dramatically extend your weakest boundaries?
- Based on your current list, whose life are you living?
- Who can help you with this list?

Client Application

1. When would you have a "What are you putting up with?" discussion with your client?
2. What questions would you use to bring their tolerations to the surface?
3. What are indicators your clients should work on their tolerations?

EXPERIENCING GOD

A frequent dilemma reported by many in ministry is the challenge of regularly experiencing God. In fact, many recent surveys of those in ministry report that professional ministry has had a negative (at times destructive) impact on their personal relationship with God.

Sounds like many in ministry can relate to Ezekiel's dry bones in the Old Testament.

A strong personal foundation includes regular, fresh experiences of God.

A Candid Assessment. Let's begin with a candid and honest assessment. Consider the following questions:

- When was the last time you personally experienced the amazing love of God?
- On a scale of 1 to 10, how would you rate your relationship between you and the Divine?

- Review your schedule for the past 30 days. What percentage of your time was spent "doing" versus "being"?

Experiencing God. Moving forward. Consider the following questions:

- What is God's invitation to you today? Right now!
- What is needed for real change to happen in this area?
- What (or Who) keeps getting in the way?
- What habits, resources and disciplines would best support your regularly experiencing God? Other supports?

Client Application

1. What steps can you take, as a coach, to encourage candid conversation about your coachees experience of God?
2. What would be the signs and signals that your coachee is feeling a lot like Ezekiel's dry bones?
3. What words of caution would you offer to those coaching people in this area?
4. What additional resources and insights would you offer someone who can't remember the last time that they experienced God?

Resources

RESOURCE A: THE EIGHT BUILDING BLOCKS OF COACHING — A REVIEW AND QUICK REFERENCE GUIDE

This document is intended to be used as a "Quick Reference Guide" and as a tool for review of the Eight Building Blocks of Coaching.

Brief points about all eight Building Blocks are included here. For complete coverage of all Building Blocks, refer to the earlier section in this book titled *"The Eight Building Blocks of Coaching."*

1. Deep Listening

Listening is defined as:

- Being curious about the other person.
- Quieting your own mind chatter so that you can be fully present with another person.
- Creating a safe space for someone to explore.
- Conveying value. *You are important to me!*
- Not about giving answers, but exploring possibilities.
- Reflecting back, like a mirror, what you experienced from the person.
- *Really getting another person.*

What to listen for:

- Listen within the context vs. content only.
- Listen for values, beliefs, frustrations, what is said vs. what is not said.
- Listen for limiting beliefs and false assumptions.

Challenges of Listening:

- Quieting the mind or "Mind Chatter".
- Thinking about what to say next.
- Discomfort with silence.
- I'm too busy to listen.

2. Powerful Questions

One of a coach's greatest tools is the use of POWERFUL QUESTIONS. Powerful Questions promote the exploration of new possibilities and stimulate creativity. They place the individual or team in a place of responsibility. They empower individuals and teams to consider what is right for them.

Powerful Questions are:

- Directly connected to deep listening. Really getting what the other person is saying enables the Coach to craft the most effective question.
- Brief. They are laser and to the point.
- Without judgment. There is no hidden agenda. It's not leading or suggestive.
- Usually open-ended. Promoting further conversation and gathering of information.
- They help clarify and slow down the automatic responses and thinking.
- Powerful Questions invite us to shift our perspective.

What are the different types of questions?

- Questions that help the person gain perspective and understanding.
- Questions that evoke discovery.
- Questions that promote clarity and learning.
- Questions that call for action.

3. Artful Language

Language is the vehicle by which we express ourselves and help others do the same. Language has the potential to create a positive impact and propel us forward. Language also has the potential to derail and inflict great harm. Artful Language includes an awareness and further development of our own language and an awareness of the other person's language.

Artful Language includes:

- Word Choices
- Alignment of Language
- Metaphors, stories and quotes
- Distinctions
- Acknowledging

4. Action and Accountability

Action and accountability play a significant role in coaching. One of the primary reasons that a person decides to work with a coach is that they want someone to help them take action and reach their goals. This part of the coaching process has several components: brainstorming, designing the action, and follow through.

Brainstorming:
- Helicoptering
- Defining the Bull's Eye
- Identifying limiting beliefs and false assumptions
- Truth Telling
- Seeding
- Stretch

Designing the Action:
- Baby Steps
- Backward Planning
- Doing-It-Now

Follow-Through:
- Acknowledging
- Creating structure
- Strategizing
- Anchoring
- Designing Blitz Days
- Identify daily action

5. Coaching Relationship

In coaching, the three most important things are: relating, relating and relating. The Coaching Relationship is the vehicle of change and transformation.

The benefits of relating well to someone include:

- The likelihood of success increases.
- Your effectiveness as a Coach increases.
- The likelihood that a prospective Coachee will want you to coach them increases.

Components of the Coaching Relationship are:

- Trust and Intimacy
- Coaching Presence

6. Coaching Agreement

The Coaching Agreement is comprised of both initial components and an ongoing nature. The ongoing nature of the Coaching Agreement includes:

- Helping the Coachee gain clarity about what they want to focus on in that particular coaching session, as well as what they want to take away.
- As the coaching session unfolds, further clarifying and exploring the take away throughout the coaching session.
- Holding side-by-side the initial need that brought them to coaching and the current focus/take away. *Because coaching is discovery-based, not outcome-based, new insights and perspectives need to be integrated into the Coaching Agreement.*

7. Creating New Awareness

Creating New Awareness is about *raising the blinds* and letting in the light of additional information, perspective and intention. New awareness is fostered when:

- Curiosity is encouraged.
- Clarifying questions are raised.
- Beliefs and assumptions are articulated and verified.
- You intentionally walk to the other side of the room to gain a different perspective.
- You are open to other ways of viewing and interpreting the same situation.

New Awareness is facilitated by:

- Listening on multiple levels.
- Contextual Listening.
- Drilling down.
- Listening for clues.

Eliminating Limiting Beliefs and False Assumptions

- What do you want to achieve?
- What might you be assuming that is stopping you from achieving your goal?
- Articulate the POSITIVE OPPOSITE of your limiting belief or false assumption.

- Ask the Incisive Question.
- Write down the action you will take.

8. Direct Communication

Direct Communication is the ability to communicate effectively during the coaching process, using language that will have the greatest positive impact on the person being coached.

Characteristics of Direct Communication:

- Clear and laser.
- In the moment (timely).
- Constructive and judgment free.
- Appropriate silence and pauses. Authentic.
- Demonstrates a mastery of language.
- Does not stack questions.
- Does not step over things.

Four specific forms of Direct Communication include:

- The Art of Interrupting
- Advising
- Directing
- Messaging

RESOURCE B: COACHING EVALUATION FORM

Coaching Evaluation Form

Coaching4Clergy

Coach:

Coachee:

Observer:

Date:

Directions: Use the *Eight Building Blocks Evaluation Form* as your guide for providing feedback to other coaches. Please share your comments and observations.

Eight Building Blocks of Coaching

1. DEEP LISTENING	• Listened without judgment, criticism or agenda.
	• Listened without thinking about what you will be saying next.
	• Listened for values, frustrations, motivation and needs.
	• Listened for the greatness in the person you are coaching.
	• Listened for limiting beliefs and false assumptions.
	• Listened for *shoulds, oughts* and *musts.*
	• Listened for the obvious.
	• Notice the tone, pace, volume, inflection and frequently used words.

STRENGTHS

OPPORTUNITIES

2. POWERFUL QUESTIONS	• Promoted the exploration of new possibilities and stimulated creativity.
	• Placed coachee in the position of responsibility.
	• Empowered coachee to consider what is right for them.
	• Brief, laser-like and to the point.
	• Without judgment.
	• No hidden agenda.
	• Not leading or suggestive.
	• Usually open-ended.
	• Questions promoted further conversation and gathering of information.
	• Questions assisted in clarifying and slowing down automatic responses and thinking.
	• Questions provided a shift in perspective.

STRENGTHS

OPPORTUNITIES

3. ARTFUL LANGUAGE	• Used clean, neutral, non-manipulative and agenda-less language.
	• Used language that goes below the surface to the core issue(s).
	• Matched the words/phrases of the coachee and knew when to introduce new words.
	• Matched the pace and pattern of the coachee.
	• Used language to help coachee learn, describe their values and define their reality.
	• Intentionally aligned language to convey acceptance and that you "get them."
	• Intentionally misaligned language as a way of calling attention to a specific issue.

STRENGTHS

OPPORTUNITIES

4. ACTION AND ACCOUNTABILITY	• Helped coachee discover different perspectives and possibilities.
• Encouraged coachee to rise above their current situation and see bigger picture.
• Helped *coachee define what* success looks like.
• Raised awareness of new ideas and nurtured current ideas.
• Challenged coachee to stretch themselves.
• Assisted coachee in designing their actions with measurable outcomes.
• Encouraged a "do it now" attitude.
• Assisted coachee in developing an action plan.
• Assisted coachee in identifying how they will stay focused on the task at hand.
• Identify barriers that might derail forward progress.

STRENGTHS

OPPORTUNITIES

5. COACHING RELATIONSHIP	• Provided a safe and supportive environment.
	• Genuine concern was demonstrated.
	• Provided a space for the coachee to be "real", where they can share, risk and explore without fear of judgment or rejection.
	• Trust is modeled.
	• The coach worked to go "deeper" with the coaching to the core issues.
	• The coach provided their full attention to the coachee.
	• The coach was in constant discovery mode.
	• The coach was open to not knowing and was comfortable "dancing" with the coachee.
	• Humor was used effectively.
	• The coach did not get enmeshed in the coachee's issues and challenges.

STRENGTHS

OPPORTUNITIES

6. COACHING AGREEMENT	• Asked coachee to articulate their desire/goal for the coaching session.
	• Used paraphrasing with coachee to ensure understanding.
	• Helped coachee gain clarity about what they wanted to focus on during the coaching session.
	• Asked coachee to define the "take away" they wanted from the coaching session.
	• Further clarified and explored the "take away" throughout the coaching session.
	• Was flexible in changing focus if conversation necessitated a change in direction.
	• Held side-by-side the initial need that brought them to coaching and the current focus/take away.

STRENGTHS

OPPORTUNITIES

7. CREATING NEW AWARENESS	• Curiosity was demonstrated and encouraged.
	• Clarifying questions were used to further explore topics and uncover new insights.
	• Beliefs and assumptions were articulated, questioned and verified.
	• The coach intentionally offered a new/different perspective for the coachee to consider.
	• The coach opened up other ways of viewing and interpreting the same situation.

STRENGTHS

OPPORTUNITIES

8. DIRECT COMMUNICATION	• Clear and laser.
	• In the moment (timely).
	• Authentic, constructive and judgment free.
	• Appropriate silence and pauses.
	• Did not stack questions.
	• Did not "step-over" issues/topics.
	• Interrupted appropriately and with respect.

8. DIRECT COMMUNICATION (CONT.)	• When interrupting, asked for permission. *May I interrupt you?* Bottom-lined it for the coachee. *Here's what I'm hearing…* • Gave advice as an educated, experienced opinion only after all other options had been explored. *Here's what I've seen work. Tell me if it sounds like it's worth experimenting with.* • Re-focused or steered the coachee back toward their goals, when needed. • When appropriate, the coach reminded them of the importance of what they are doing and where they are going. • "Truth told"— coach told it like they saw it. • Acknowledged the coachee and tapped into their greatness. • Coach endorsed what the coachee had accomplished. • Advised them on what was next. *You probably need to start focusing on ABC, because you've moved past XYZ.* • Coach told them what they wanted for them. *"What I want for you is…"*

STRENGTHS

OPPORTUNITIES

OVERALL COMMENTS

RESOURCE C: SAMPLE WELCOME KIT

Sample Welcome Letter

Welcome and Congratulations!!!

Thank you for deciding to begin the coaching process and for choosing me as your coach. My commitment is to provide you with the best possible coaching that I can.

In order for you to get the most out of your coaching sessions, I am sending you a number of items for you to read before your first coaching session. These items include:

- **A Coaching Agreement.** My request is that you read this contract, sign it and return it to me.
- **Contact information.** This information is kept private.
- **Code of Ethics.** I am a member of the International Coach Federation and I have signed an agreement to abide by their Code of Ethics.
- **First Coaching Session Form.** I ask that you complete and return this to me prior to your first coaching session.
- **Focus Report.** This is a quick and simple report that I ask you to complete and return to me prior to each coaching session (excluding your first coaching session). Completion of this form not only helps you prepare for each coaching session, but also prepares me as your coach.

At the time of the agreed upon coaching session, I ask you to call me at <**Your Telephone Number**>. Each session is approximately 30 minutes in length. Since I have clients before and after each coaching session, it is important that we adhere to the 30 minute timeframe.

Occasionally, between coaching sessions, you may want to call or e-mail me. Please feel free to do either. My commitment is to respond to you in a timely manner, as time permits.

Again, welcome to the coaching process and congratulations on taking this important step forward.

<**Your Name Here**>

Sample Agreement

Coaching Agreement

To my client: Please review, adjust, sign where indicated, and return to me at the address listed below.

NAME

INITIAL TERM   MONTH, FROM   THROUGH

FEE $ PER MONTH

NUMBER OF SESSIONS PER MONTH

DURATION   (length of scheduled session)

REFERRED BY:

GROUND RULES: 1. CLIENT CALLS THE COACH AT THE SCHEDULED TIME.

                      2. CLIENT PAYS COACHING FEES IN ADVANCE.

                      3. CLIENT PAYS FOR LONG-DISTANCE CHARGES, IF ANY.

1. As a client, I understand and agree that I am fully responsible for my physical, mental and emotional well-being during my coaching calls, including my choices and decisions. I am aware that I can choose to cancel this coaching agreement at any time upon 30 days written notice.

2. I understand that "coaching" is a Professional-Client relationship I have with my coach that is designed to facilitate the creation/development of personal, professional or business goals and to develop and carry out a strategy/plan for achieving those goals.

3. I understand that coaching is a comprehensive process that may involve all areas of my life, including work, finances, health, relationships, education and recreation. I acknowledge that deciding how to handle these issues, incorporating coaching into those areas, and implementing my choices is exclusively my responsibility.

4. I understand that coaching does not involve the diagnosis or treatment of mental disorders as defined by the American Psychiatric Association. I understand that coaching is not a substitute for counseling, psychotherapy, psychoanalysis, mental health care or substance abuse treatment and I will not use it in place of any form of diagnosis, treatment or therapy.

5. I promise that if I am currently in therapy or otherwise under the care of a mental health professional, I have consulted with the mental health care provider regarding

the advisability of working with a coach and that this person is aware of my decision to proceed with the coaching relationship.

6. I understand that information will be held as confidential unless I state otherwise, in writing, except as required by law.

7. I understand that certain topics may be anonymously and hypothetically shared with other coaching professionals for training OR consultation purposes.

8. I understand that coaching is not to be used as a substitute for professional advice by legal, medical, financial, business, spiritual or other qualified professionals. I will seek independent professional guidance for legal, medical, financial, business, spiritual or other matters. I understand that all decisions in these areas are exclusively mine and I acknowledge that my decisions and my actions regarding them are my sole responsibility.

I have read and agree to the above.

_____

Client Signature

Date:

Please return to:

_____

Sample Contact Form

Contact Information

*(Please forward this information to me at <**Your Email Address Here**>)*

Name:

Address:

Telephone Numbers: (Best way to reach you)

Primary:

Secondary:

Other:

Email Address:

Would you like to receive my monthly e-newsletter?   Yes   No

Name of your ministry setting and your role:

Sample First Coaching Session Form

First Coaching Session

Please answer the following questions and e-mail your responses to me at least one day before your first coaching session.

1. What are 10 things I **absolutely** need to know about you and your church?

    1. _____

    2. _____

    3. _____

    4. _____

    5. _____

    6. _____

    7. _____

    8. _____

    9. _____

    10._____

2. What do you want to be able to say about yourself, or your church, three months from now that you cannot currently say?

One year from now?

Three years from now?

3. Why is this important to you?

4. What is holding you back? What keeps getting in the way?

5. What is one simple thing you could do to get closer to your goal?
   (Right now! Today! This week!)

Sample Focus Report Form

Focus Report

Name: Date:

Please call <Your Telephone Number Here> **for your coaching sessions**

What I have accomplished OR what action I have taken since our last session.

What I did not accomplish but intended to do AND what got in the way.

At this moment, the biggest challenges or issues I am dealing with are....

I want to focus our attention during our next coaching session on....

RESOURCE D: A LIST OF POWERFUL QUESTIONS

Top 10 Year-End Questions for You or Your Team

1. What have you accomplished this year? Be specific. Write it down. Schedule some time to celebrate this!

2. What have you learned this year? What skills did you pick up? What lessons?

3. What got in your way? Where will your work be next year? Be honest if it was you who got in the way.

4. Who contributed to your success? What can you do to recognize these members of your personal or professional team?

5. What mistakes did you make, and what did you learn from them? Writing these down is a good refresher for what not to do next year.

6. How was your work consistent with your values?

7. Where did you not take responsibility? Sometimes this is easier to see with a little distance from the actual event.

8. How did your performance rate? Give yourself a letter grade or a 1 to 10 score.

9. What do you need to let go of? Doing so can help you move much more lightly into the New Year.

10. What was missing for you this year? How can you incorporate it into next year?

Top 10 Questions for Leaders

1. What do you want to be able to say three years from now that you can't say today (about yourself or your organization)?

2. What are the possible next steps?

3. Who can help you with this?

4. What's the truth about now?

5. How do you handle failure?

6. What do you model?

7. How much of a people pleaser are you?

8. What do you need to say goodbye to in order to move forward?

9. On a scale of 1 to 10 how committed are you to taking action?
    (1= no commitment, 10=high commitment)

10. What's the payoff of not taking action?

Val's Favorite Questions

1. What's next?

2. What do you want?

3. What are you afraid of?

4. What is this costing you?

5. What are you attached to?

6. What is the dream?

7. What is the essence of the dream?

8. What is beyond this problem?

9. What is ahead?

10. What are you building towards?

11. What has to happen for you to feel successful?

12. What gift are you not being responsible for?

13. What are your healthy sources of energy?

14. What stops you?

15. What's stopping you?

16. What's in your way?

17. What would make the biggest difference here?

18. What are you going to do?

19. What do you like to do?

20. What can you do to be happy right now?

21. What do you hope to accomplish by having that conversation?

22. What do you hope to accomplish by doing that?

23. What's the first step?

24. What would it be like to have excitement and fear at the same time?

25. What's important about that?

26. What would it take for you to treat yourself like your best client?

27. What benefit/payoff is there in the present situation?

28. What do you expect to have happen?

29. What's the ideal?

30. What's the ideal outcome?

31. What would it look like?

32. What's the truth about this situation?

33. What's the right action?

34. What are you going to do?

35. What's working for you?

36. What would you do differently?

37. What decision would you make from a place of abundance?

38. What other choices do you have?

39. What do you really, really want?

40. What if there were no limits?

41. What aren't you telling me that's keeping me from coaching/helping you?

42. What haven't I asked that I should ask?

43. What needs to be said that has not been said?

44. What are you not saying?

45. What else do you have to say about that?

46. What is left to do to have this be complete?

47. What do you have invested in continuing to do it this way?

48. What is that?

49. What comes first?

50. What consequence are you avoiding?

51. What is the value you received from this meeting/conversation?

52. What is motivating you?

53. What has you hooked?

54. What is missing here?

55. What does that remind you of?

56. What do you suggest?

57. What is underneath that?

58. What part of what I said was useful? And how so?

59. What is this person contributing to the quality of your life?

60. What is it that you are denying yourself right now?

61. What do you need to put in place to accomplish this?

62. What is the simplest solution here?

63. What would help you know I support this/you completely?

64. What happened?

65. What are you avoiding?

66. What is the worst that could happen?

67. What are you committed to?

68. What is your vision for yourself and the people around you?

69. What don't you want?

70. What if you knew?

71. What's your heart telling you? What are you willing to give up?

72. What might you have done differently?

73. What are you not facing?

74. What does this feeling remind you of?

75. What would you do differently if this problem were solved?

76. What does your soul say?

77. What do you need to say goodbye to in order to move forward?

78. What's the payoff for you of not dealing with this issue?

79. Are things as bad as you say they are or are they worse?

80. At what point when you say "yes" are you really feeling "no"?

81. What is the decision you are avoiding?

82. What are you pretending not to know?

83. What are ten things I absolutely need to know about you?

84. What do you want to be able to say about yourself (your church) three months from now? One year from now? Three years from now?

85. What is holding you back? What keeps getting in the way?

86. What is one simple thing you could do today to get you closer to your goal? (Right now! Today!)

87. What is your biggest, wildest dream?

88. What keeps you up at night? What do you find yourself continually thinking about when you're in the shower?

89. What has motivated you in the past to reach/achieve difficult goals, make important decisions, or do challenging things? Can we use this as a motivator now?

90. Who can help you with this?

91. What are you tolerating?

92. What has served you in the past? Is it still in effect now?

93. What would you do if you knew you couldn't fail?

94. What part of this goal is yours? What belongs to someone else? What if the goal was all yours?

95. How can I best support you? What do you need most from me?

96. What are you grateful for?

97. What makes your heart sing?

98. What's missing?

99. What do you have to do differently to make this happen?

100. What do you need to put in place to make this happen?

101. When you attain your goal, what will it look like?

102. Who do you know that is already doing this well?

103. What will be the signs that it's time to begin?

104. How will you know that you have succeeded?

105. How will you know when you arrive?

106. What about yourself do you need to change?

107. What is one thing you need to focus on to get where you want to go?

108. Could you be mistaken? How could you check this out?

109. Does this align with your vision and goals?

110. What is one thing you feel really good about over this past week?

111. What one thing would make the biggest difference right now?

112. What's your belief about this situation?

113. What would you like more of? Less of?

114. What is true about this situation?

115. What are the affects of this on you?

116. What steps would move this forward?

117. How attached are you to the outcome?

118. What is the "should" in this situation?

119. Is this the time to begin?

120. What is the truth about this situation?

121. What is the path of least resistance?

122. Is there another way? Let's brainstorm 5 to 10 other possibilities.

123. What is this costing you?

124. Can you see what is beyond this problem?

125. Can you see what's ahead?

126. Are you open to a completely different way of looking at this?

127. What are your actions saying about this situation?

128. What will happen if you keep doing this for the next 10 years?

129. Underneath all of this, what are you really committed to?

130. What is the legacy that you want to leave behind?

131. May I push you on this?

132. So, what's possible here?

133. What opportunities are you not taking advantage of?

134. Who's really in charge here?

135. What are five changes or actions that you can take in the next 30 days that will move you forward?

136. What are you willing to do to make this work?

137. What consumes your time, to the point that it distracts you from attaining your goals?

138. What do you really, really, really, REALLY want?

139. What are you afraid of about this situation?

140. What is the worst that could happen? And if that happened, what's the worst that could happen after that?

141. What is the best that could happen?

142. What are you NOT saying? What are you holding back?

143. Are you pursuing a goal that no longer makes sense?

144. What internal rules and unspoken standards are having a negative impact?

RESOURCE E: ADDITIONAL COACHING TECHNIQUES AND STRATEGIES

We've included in this text a number of exercises and techniques that you can use in your coaching.

Focus Exercise

This exercise helps the individual gain clarity about their primary roles and responsibilities.

Begin by writing your responses to each of these questions:

1. What are the things that only you can do?

2. What are the things that you and others can do?

3. What are the things that you can do, but choose not to do?

4. What are the things that you cannot do and never want to do?

Look over your answers and deepen your learning with these additional questions:

- How does what you have written compare with how you actually spend your time and energy?

- What would it take to spend the majority of your time doing what only you can do?

- Who do you need to be in order to make this a reality?

Identify the changes and adjustments necessary and take action now. Today.

Leadership Timetable

In order to respond to the challenges of leadership, leaders must make time for these priorities:

- Rest: Every good leader understands the importance of taking care of their physical body. (Also see Power Sabbath below.)

- Results: Make time for your main goals.

- Response: Make sure there is adequate time for follow-up and follow-through.

- Refocus: Schedule time for course corrections and fine-tuning.

Ask your coachees which of the four "R's" they frequently forget. The final "R" is often the most overlooked. Then ask, "Which of these "R's" would be of the greatest benefit to you and your leadership?"

Take a Power Sabbath

A Power Sabbath includes four areas of rest. They include:

1. Physical Rest: Make sure your body is getting adequate rest.
2. Mind Rest: Enjoy some silence. Turn off the TV. Take a break from reading the depressing news in the paper. Just let your mind rest.
3. Heart Rest: Caring for others and their needs can become exhausting. Take a short break and let others care for you. You'll be better able to care for others when you return.
4. Soul Rest: Take time to experience the divine. Rest in the knowledge that the world revolves around God, not you or me!

When traveling by airplane, we're reminded that in an emergency, those traveling with children are to put on their own oxygen mask first and then care for their children. A strong personal foundation is like putting on your oxygen mask first. You are then better able to care for and lead those around you.

A "Dear John" Letter

This humorous yet powerful letter can be presented to a client to demonstrate the impact of not changing.

Dear John,

You probably already know what this letter is about. You've seen it coming; I know you have. It's about us, John. It's over. I'm leaving you!

I've hung on as long as I could. You've got to give me credit for that. I mean, the way you swept me off my feet and talked lovingly about the future we would have together. I have waited so long for your embrace, your attention, and your love.

Why have you neglected me? Why have you made so many excuses? Your inaction and addiction to procrastination is tearing me apart. I simply must move on!

For years, I would get so excited every time you talked about getting started. My heart would pitter-patter every time you talked about me to other people, only to be let down once again because you were afraid. John, what are you afraid of? It's only me! I am your hopes, dreams, and goals. I wanted you as much as you wanted me, but you have left me no choice. I simply must move on!

Please do not attempt to talk your way out of this. The years of indecision and lack of discipline tell me everything I need to know. If you really—and I mean REALLY—wanted me, you would have found a way for us to be together.

I am tired of having my hopes soar so high just to see them dashed. I simply must move on! Time is marching by without us, and my greatest fear is suddenly becoming visible on the horizon. I am so afraid that we could come to the end of our lifetime and never have the chance to really know one another. It breaks my heart to even entertain this thought, but I simply must move on!

All I wanted, needed, and asked for was your attention, your devotion, and your willingness to work hard for me. If that was too much to ask for, then I'm sorry. I simply must move on! All things of value must be earned, and I've grown tired of your excuses and lack of patience. On numerous occasions, I was within your grasp, but you quit too soon. Why did you leave me when you were so close?

I've grown tired of hearing that the timing is not right, that you're tired, or that someday you'll get around to it. It's now time that I get around to it myself and find someone who is committed, focused, and proactive. I simply must move on!

Sincerely,

Your hopes and dreams and goals for the past year

Split Time Versus Solid Time

A common challenge among coaching clients is getting things done, especially those items that only they can do. The To-Do list keeps growing. Feelings of guilt and inadequacy take root. The latest technological gismos are of no assistance. No matter what, there still aren't enough hours in the week to do all you want and need to do.

If you look more closely at your tasks and what they require, you can get past this bottleneck in no time. You see, some tasks require a solid block of time to be completed. These items often require a creative flow of thought or have a sequence/strategic process to them. Every time you stop and re-start a solid block project, you lose valuable time and momentum.

Split-time tasks, on the other hand, can be stopped and restarted with little to no loss of time or momentum. These kinds of tasks can be worked on when you discover a few extra minutes or when you're on auto-pilot.

Give this a try: Begin by identifying what you need to do in any given week. Then, for each task, decide if you need a "solid" block of time OR a "split" block of time.

You will be amazed at how this simple distinction will allow you to use your time so much more efficiently, and how much more quickly you will complete the tasks on your list.

References

The International Coach Federation. http://www.coachfederation.org.

Kline, Nancy. *Time to Think*. London: Cassell Illustrated, 1999.

NIV Pastor's Bible. Grand Rapids: Zondervan Publishing House, 2000.

Pawlik-Kienlen, Laurie. *Protecting Personal Boundaries*. 2006.

Peterson, Eugene. *The Message*. Colorado Springs: Navpress Publishing Group, 1995.

Stull, Craig, Phil Myers and David Meerman Scott. *Tuned In*. New Jersey: John Wiley & Sons, Inc., 2008.

Scholtes, Peter R. et al. *The TEAM Handbook*. Madison, Wisconsin: Oriel, Inc., 2003.

Winesman, Albert L., Donald O. Clifton, and Curt Liesveld. *Living Your Strengths*. New York: Gallup Press, 2003-2004.

Zander, Rosamund Stone and Benjamin Zander. *The Art of Possibility*. Penguin Books, Ltd., London, England, 2000.

About the Author

J. Val Hastings, MCC, is the Founder and President of Coaching4Clergy, which provides specialized training for pastors, church leaders and coaches. Val hired his first coach while he was pastoring at a local United Methodist church. His progress was noticeable by all, and he began to wonder, "What if I adopted a coaching approach to ministry? What if the larger church adopted a coaching approach to ministry?" In that moment, a vision began to emerge – a global vision of Every Pastor, Ministry Staff and Church Leader a Coach.

Val is the author of the book The Next Great Awakening: How to Empower God's People with a Coach Approach to Ministry and the e-book The E3-Church: Empowered, Effective and Entrepreneurial Leadership That Will Keep Your Church Alive. Val currently holds the designation of Master Certified Coach through the International Coach Federation, its highest coaching designation.

16720191R00077

Made in the USA
Charleston, SC
07 January 2013